T0209203

THE INFORMATION BOMB

THE INFORMATION BOMB

Paul Virilio

Translated by Chris Turner

VERSO

London • New York

Originally published as *La Bombe informatique* by Editions Galileé, Paris 1998
© Editions Galilée 1998
Translation first published by Verso 2000
© Chris Turner 2000
This edition published by Verso 2005

5 7 9 10 8 6 4

Verso
UK: 6 Meard Street, London W1F 0EG
USA: 20 Jay Street, Suite 1010, Brooklyn, NY 11201
www.versobooks.com

Verso is the imprint of New Left Books

ISBN 978-1-84477-059-8

British Library Cataloguing in Publication Data
A catalogue record for this book is available from the British Library

Library of Congress Cataloging-in-Publication Data
A catalog record for this book is available from the Library of Congress

Printed and Bound in the United States

No one can say what will be 'real' for people when the wars which are now beginning come to an end.

Werner Heisenberg

Some of these pieces appeared between 1996 and 1998 in three newspapers: the *Frankfurter Rundschau*, the *Tagesanzeiger* of Zürich, and *Der Standard* of Vienna.

Translator's
Acknowledgements

I would like to thank Glynis Powell and Marie-Dominique Maison for their assistance in the preparation of this translation. Thanks are also due, as ever, to the inter-library loan department of Birmingham City Library and, more unusually, to the Atuagkat Bookstore in Nuuk, Greenland.

CHAPTER 1

The civilianization or militarization of science?

If truth is what is verifiable, the truth of contemporary science is not so much the extent of progress achieved as the scale of technical catastrophes occasioned.

Science, after having been carried along for almost half a century in the arms race of the East–West deterrence era, has developed solely with a view to the pursuit of *limit-performances*, to the detriment of any effort to discover a coherent truth useful to humanity.

Modern science, having progressively become **technoscience** – the product of the fatal confusion between the *operational instrument* and *exploratory research* – has slipped its philosophical moorings and lost its way, without anyone taking umbrage at this, except for a few ecological and religious leaders.[1]

---

1 Pope John Paul II was criticizing the militarization of science and its culture of death as early as the late 1980s.

Indeed, if the 'experience of thought' does in fact lie at the origin of the experimental sciences, we cannot but notice today the decline of that *analogue* mental process, in favour of instrumental, *digital* procedures, which are capable, we are told, of boosting knowledge.

Operational reality of the technical instrument, *resolutory* truth of scientific thought – two fundamentally distinct aspects of knowledge, which are fused here without anyone apparently becoming alerted to the situation.

Science, which is not so attached to 'truth' as once it was, but more to immediate 'effectiveness', is now drifting towards its decline, its civic fall from grace . . . . As a panic phenomenon – a fact concealed by the success of its devices and tools – contemporary science is losing itself in the very excessiveness of its alleged progress. Much as a strategic offensive can wear itself out by the scale of its tactical conquests, so techno-science is gradually wrecking the scholarly resources of all knowledge.

Like an Olympic sport in which the performance drugs, the anabolic steroids and such like, destroy the meaning of the athletes' effort by an abuse of the pharmacopoeia, *extreme science* is moving away from patient research into reality to become part of a phenomenon of generalized virtualization.

After having been drawn, against its own better nature, into the planetary death race of the 'balance of terror', 'post-modern' science is now engaging in a new type of competition that is equally insane: *a race to achieve limit-performances in the fields of robotics or genetic engineering*, which in its turn draws the various scientific disciplines on to the path of a 'post-scientific extremism' that exiles them from all reason.

Science, which was once a rigorous field thriving on intellectual adventure, is today bogged down in a technological adventurism that denatures it. 'Science of the excess', of extremes – a limit-science or the limit of science?

As everyone knows, that which is excessive is insignificant. 'Science without conscience is mere ruination of the soul' (Rabelais), and a techno-science without a consciousness of its impending end is, however unwittingly, merely a sport.

'Extreme sports' – those in which one deliberately risks one's life on the pretext of achieving a record performance.

'Extreme science' – the science which runs the incalculable risk of the disappearance of all science. As the tragic phenomenon of a knowledge which has suddenly become **cybernetic**, this techno-science becomes, then, as mass techno-culture, the agent not, as in the past, of the acceleration of history, but of the dizzying whirl of *the acceleration of reality* – and that to the detriment of all verisimilitude.

Only a few centuries after having been, with Copernicus and Galileo, the *science of the appearance* of a relative truth, techno-science is once again becoming a *science of the disappearance* of that same truth with the coming of a knowledge which is not so much encyclopaedic as cybernetic, a knowledge which denies all objective reality.

Thus, after having largely contributed to speeding up the various means for the representation of the world, with optics, electro-optics and even the recent establishment of the space of virtual reality, contemporary sciences are engaging, *a contrario*, in the eclipsing of the real, in the aesthetics of scientific disappearance.

A *science of verisimilitude, of the plausible*, still attached to the discovery of a relative truth? Or a *science of implausibility*, committed today to the research and development of a heightened virtual reality? This is the alternative we are offered.

In fact, the only scientific horizon is authenticity, the experimental rigour of researchers. Unfortunately, we know what media abuses surround certain 'discoveries'. We know the promotional character of the premature announcement of the results of a particular experiment, when what is really going on is little more than an exercise in the conditioning of public opinion by an extremist science. That science is now concerned less with truth than with the effect created by the announcement of a new discovery – though not, as used to be the case, a genuine discovery serving the common good.

In illustration of these disenchanted remarks, we may usefully criticize the carefully sustained confusion between the *sporting hero* and the *scientist*, between the adventurer who pushes himself violently to his *physical* limits and the white-coated adventurer who pushes himself to the *ethical* limits, the adventurer who experiences the elation of risking not just his own death, but that of the human race.

Let us examine, for example, the Bob Dent–Philip Nitschke affair. On Thursday 26 September 1996, Bob Dent, a cancer patient in his sixties, was the first person to make use of an Australian law which had been in force since 1 July of the same year: the so-called Terminal Act.[2]

---

2 The Northern Territory's Rights of the Terminally Ill Act remained in force until 27 March 1997, when it was overturned by the Australian federal government. (Trans.)

Linked to a computer managing his IV system, Dent said 'yes' a first time to the machine developed by his doctor, Philip Nitschke.

After a period of nine days, as laid down by law, he clicked on 'yes' a second time. The choice before him at that point was: 'If you click on "yes", a lethal injection will be administered within thirty seconds and you will die.'

From these facts taken as a whole – *nine months* to be born without any choice in the matter, *nine days* to die voluntarily, *thirty seconds* to change your mind – there arises the question of the limits of science, of a science which is here akin to therapeutic extinction. Is this the science of programmed decease or *computer-aided suicide*?

There is much to be said about this 'decisional death', in which the doctor's participation is confined to developing *a buck-passing machine*, the cause of active euthanasia advancing behind the mask of a cybernetic procedure for inflicting sudden death.

A clinical example of the new virtualization of action, in which *remote electronic action* wipes away the patient's guilt, together with the scientist's responsibility.

Philip Nitschke, innocent of the crime of active euthanasia, and no more responsible than a dealer in firearms or knives, has managed to take advantage not just of the ambiguity of the aptly named 'Terminal Act', but of the nihilism of the coming cybernetic era.

Like Kasparov, the world chess champion, playing a game against a computer specially designed to defeat him, Philip Nitschke has just pioneered the creation of a new 'fatal' couple.

Let us not forget, however, that what took place

between the doctor and his 'patient' – impatient, as it happens, to put an end to his life – had already been in play in the age of the balance of programmed terror, with the system of 'Mutually Assured Destruction' (MAD) between East and West, and the development – interrupted by the implosion of the Soviet Union – of a genuine 'doomsday machine' capable of deciding the passive euthanasia of humanity by automatically triggering the nuclear apocalypse.

CHAPTER 2

Totality or all-inclusiveness? We can scarcely avoid the question today of what is meant by the endlessly repeated word **globalization**. Is this a term intended to take over from the word **internationalism**, associated too closely with communism, or, as is often claimed, is it a reference to single-market capitalism?

Either answer is wide of the mark. After the 'end of history', prematurely announced a few years ago by Francis Fukuyama,[1] what is being revealed here are the beginnings of the 'end of the space' of a small planet held in suspension in the electronic ether of our modern means of telecommunication.

Let us not forget that 'excellence is a completion' (Aristotle), and perfect accomplishment a definitive conclusion.

---

1 Francis Fukuyama, *The End of History and the Last Man*, Hamish Hamilton, London, 1992.

The time of the finite world is coming to an end and, unless we are astronomers or geophysicists, we shall understand nothing of the sudden 'globalization of history' if we do not go back to physics and the reality of the moment.

To claim, as is now the case, that **globalism** illustrates the victory of free enterprise over totalitarian collectivism is to understand nothing of the current loss of time intervals, the endless feedback, the telescoping of industrial or post-industrial activities.

How are we to conceive the change wrought by computerization if we remain tied to an ideological approach, when the urgent need is in fact for a new geostrategic approach to discover the scale of the phenomenon that is upon us? And we need to do this *to come back to the Earth* – not in the sense of the old earth which sustains and nourishes us, but of the unique celestial body we occupy. To return to the world, *to its dimensions* and to the coming loss of those dimensions in the acceleration not now of history (which, with the loss of local time, has just lost its concrete foundations), but of reality itself, with the new-found importance of this world time, a time whose instantaneity definitively cancels the reality of distances – the reality of those geographical intervals which only yesterday still organized the politics of nations and their alliances, the importance of which had been shown by the Cold War in the age of (East/West) bloc politics.

'Physics' and 'metaphysics' are two terms which have been current in philosophy and understood in that discipline since Aristotle, but what of *geophysics* and *meta-geophysics*? There is still doubt over the meaning of the latter term, while the factual reality clearly shows that the continents have lost their geographical foundations and been supplanted by the *tele-continents* of a global communication system which has become quasi-instantaneous.

After the extreme political importance assumed by the geophysics of the globe over the history of societies separated not so much by their national frontiers as by communications distances and timelags, we have in recent times seen the transpolitical importance of this kind of *meta-geophysics* which the cybernetic **interactivity** of the contemporary world represents for us at the end of the twentieth century.

Since all presence is presence only at a distance, the **tele-presence** of the era of the globalization of exchanges could only be established across the widest possible gap. This is a gap which now stretches to the other side of the world, from one edge to the other of present reality. But this is a meta-geophysical reality which strictly regulates the tele-continents of a *virtual reality* that monopolizes the greater part of the economic activity of the nations and, conversely, destroys cultures which are precisely situated in the space of the physics of the globe.

We are not seeing an 'end of history', but we are seeing an end of geography. Whereas, until the transport revolution of the nineteenth century, the old time intervals produced an auspicious distancing between the various societies, in the age of the current transmission revolution, the ceaseless feedback of human activities is generating the invisible threat of an accident befalling this generalized interactivity – an accident of which the stock market crash might be a symptom.

This point can be illustrated by a particularly significant anecdote: in the last few years, or, more precisely, since the early 1990s, the Pentagon has taken the view that *geostrategy is turning the globe inside out like a glove.*

For American military leaders, the **global** is the *interior* of a finite world whose very finitude poses many logistical problems. And the **local** is the *exterior*, the periphery, if not indeed the 'outer suburbs' of the world.

For the US general staff, then, the pips are no longer inside the apples, nor the segments in the middle of the orange: *the skin has been turned inside out.* The exterior is not simply the skin, the surface of the Earth, but all that is *in situ*, all that is precisely localized, wherever it may be.

There lies the great globalitarian transformation, the transformation which extraverts localness – all localness – and which does not now deport persons, or entire populations, as in the past, but deports their living space, the place where they subsist economically. A global de-localization, which affects the very nature not merely of 'national', but of 'social' identity, throwing into question not so much the nation-state, but the city, the geopolitics of nations.

'For the first time,' declared President Clinton, 'there is no longer any difference between domestic and foreign policy.' No longer any distinction between the outside and the inside – admittedly with the exception of the topological reversal effected previously by the Pentagon and the State Department.

In fact, this historic phrase spoken by the American president ushers in the **meta-political** dimension of a power which has become global and permits us to believe that domestic policy will now be handled as external policy was in the past.

The real city, which is situated in a precise place and

which gave its name to the politics of nations, is giving way to the *virtual city*, that de-territorialized **meta-city** which is hence to become the site of that *metropolitics*, the totalitarian or rather globalitarian character of which will be plain for all to see.

We had no doubt forgotten that alongside wealth and its accumulation, there is speed and its concentration, without which the centralization of the powers that have succeeded each other throughout history would quite simply not have taken place: feudal and monarchic power, or the power of the national state, for which the acceleration of transport and transmissions made the government of dispersed populations easier.

Today, with the new policy of trade globalization, the city is foregrounded once more. As one of humanity's major historic forms, the metropolis provides a focus for the vitality of the nations of the globe.

But this **local city** is now only a **district**, one borough among others of the invisible **world meta-city** whose 'centre is everywhere and whose circumference nowhere' (Pascal).

The virtual hypercentre, of which real cities are only ever the periphery. And, with the desertification of rural space, this phenomenon is further accentuating the decline of medium-sized towns, incapable of holding out for long against the attraction of the metropoles, which have all the telecommunications infrastructure, together with the high-speed air and rail links. The *metropolitical* phenomenon of a catastrophic human hyper-concentration that is gradually coming to suppress the urgent need for a genuine *geopolitics* of populations which were previously spread harmoniously over the whole of their territories.

To illustrate the recent consequences of domestic telecommunications for municipal politics, one last anecdote: since the sudden proliferation of mobile phones, the Los Angeles police have found themselves presented with a difficulty of a new kind. Whereas, in the past, drug dealing in its various forms was precisely situated in a number of districts that were easily monitored by the narcotics squads, those squads are now entirely defeated by the random and essentially de-localized meetings between dealers and users who all have mobile phones and can meet wherever they decide – literally, anywhere.

A single technical phenomenon which both facilitates metropolitan *concentration* and the *dispersal* of major risks – this needed to be borne in mind if, in the future (at all events, very soon), a cybernetic control appropriate to domestic networks was to be developed . . . hence the relentless advance of the Internet, the recently *civilianized* military network.

The more that time intervals are abolished, the more the image of space dilates: 'You would think that an explosion had occurred all over the planet. The least nook and cranny are dragged out of the shade by a stark light,' wrote Ernst Jünger of that illumination which lights up the reality of the world.

The coming of the 'live', of 'direct transmission', brought about by turning the limit-speed of waves to effect, transforms the old 'tele-vision' into a **planetary grand-scale optics**.

With CNN and its various offshoots, domestic television has given way to **tele-surveillance**.

This sudden **focusing** – a security-orientated phenomenon of the media monitoring of the life of nations – heralds

the dawn of a particular form of day, which totally escapes
the diurnal–nocturnal alternation that previously struc-
tured history.

With this **false day**, produced by the illumination of
telecommunications, an artificial sun rises, an emergency
lighting system which ushers in a new time: **world time**,
in which the simultaneity of actions should soon gain
precedence over their successive character.

With **visual** (audiovisual) **continuity** progressively
taking over from the **territorial contiguity** of nations,
which has now declined in importance, the political frontiers were themselves to shift from the real space of
geopolitics to the 'real time' of the chronopolitics of the
transmission of images and sounds. Two complementary
aspects of **globalization** have, then, to be taken into
account today: on the one hand, the extreme reduction of
distances which ensues from the **temporal compression**
of transport and transmissions; on the other, the current
general spread of **tele-surveillance**. A new vision of a
world that is constantly 'tele-present' twenty-four hours a
day, seven days a week, thanks to the artifice of this 'transhorizon optics' which puts what was previously out of
sight on display.

'The destiny of every image is enlargement,' declared
Gaston Bachelard. It is science, techno-science, which has
taken responsibility for this fate of images. In the past, it
did so with the telescope and the microscope. In the
future, it will do so with a domestic tele-surveillance that
will exceed the strictly military dimensions of this
phenomenon.

The exhaustion of the political importance of extension, which is a product of the unremarked pollution by

acceleration of the **life-size nature** of the terrestrial globe, demands the invention of a **substitute grand-scale optics**.

This is an *active* (wave) *optics*, replacing in a thorough-going way the *passive* (geometric) *optics* of the era of Galileo's spy-glass. And doing so as though the loss of the horizon-line of geographical perspective imperatively necessitated the establishment of a **substitute horizon**: the 'artificial horizon' of a screen or a monitor, capable of permanently displaying the new preponderance of the media perspective over the immediate perspective of space.

With the **relief** of the 'tele-present' event then taking precedence over the three dimensions of the volume of objects or places here present . . .

This helps us better to understand the sudden multipli-cation of those 'great lights'[2] that are meteorological or military observation satellites. The repeated sending into orbit of communications satellites, the spread of metro-politan video-surveillance or, alternatively, the recent development of live-cams on the Internet.

All this contributing, as we have seen, to the inversion of the usual conceptions of *inside* and *outside*.

Finally, this generalized **visualization** is the defining aspect of what is generally known today as **virtualization**.

The much-vaunted 'virtual reality' is not so much a navigation through the **cyberspace** of the networks. It is, first and foremost, the **amplification of the optical density** of the appearances of the real world.

---

2 '*Grands luminaires*': a reference to Genesis 1:16: 'And God made two great lights.'

An amplification which attempts to compensate for the contraction of distances on the Earth, a contraction brought about by the temporal compression of instantaneous telecommunications. In a world in which obligatory tele-presence is submerging the immediate presence of individuals (in work, trade, etc.), television can no longer be what it has been for half a century: a place of entertainment or of the promotion of culture; it must, first and foremost, **give birth to** the world time of exchanges, to this virtual vision which is supplanting the vision of the real world around us.

Grand-Scale Transhorizon Optics is, therefore, the site of all (strategic, economic, political . . .) virtualization. Without it, the development of **globalitarianism**, which is preparing to revive the **totalitarianisms** of the past, would be ineffective.

To provide the coming globalization with relief, with optical density, it is necessary not merely to connect up to the cybernetic networks, but, most important, to split the reality of the world in two.

As with *stereoscopy* and *stereophony*, which distinguish left from right, bass from treble, to make it easier to perceive audiovisual relief, it is essential today to effect a split in primary reality by developing a *stereo-reality*, made up on the one hand of *the actual reality* of immediate appearances and, on the other, of the *virtual reality* of media trans-appearances.

Not until this new 'reality effect' becomes generally accepted as commonplace will it be possible really to speak of **globalization**.

To manage at last to 'bring to light' an over-exposed world, a world without dead angles, without 'areas of shadow' (like the micro-video which replaces both car reversing lights and rear-view mirrors) – this is the objective of the technologies of **synthetic vision**.

Since *a picture is worth a thousand words*, the aim of multimedia is to turn our old television into a kind of **domestic telescope** for seeing, for foreseeing (in a manner not unlike present weather-forecasting) the world that lies just around the corner.

The aim is to make the computer screen the ultimate window, but a window which would not so much allow you to receive data as to view the horizon of globalization, the space of its accelerated virtualization . . .

Let us now take an example whose significance is widely misrecognized: that of 'live-cams', those video imaging devices which have been set up all over the place and which are only accessible through the Internet.

Though apparently aimless and insignificant, the phenomenon is nonetheless spreading to all parts of an increasing number of countries: from San Francisco Bay to Jerusalem's Wailing Wall, by way of the offices and apartments of a few exhibitionists, the camera enables you to discover **in real time** what is going on at the other end of the planet at that very moment.

Here the computer is no longer simply a device for consulting information sources, but an automatic *vision machine*, operating within the space of an entirely virtualized geographical reality.

Some Internet enthusiasts are even happy to *live their lives 'on screen'*. Interned in the closed circuits of the Web, they offer up their private lives for everyone to watch.

The collectivist introspection of these people, who exemplify a **universal voyeurism**, is set to expand at the speed of the single world advertising market, which is not far off now.

Advertising, which in the nineteenth century was simply the *publicizing* of a product, before becoming in the twentieth an *industry* for stimulating desire, is set in the twenty-first century to become pure *communication*. To this end it will require the unfurling of an advertising space which stretches to the horizon of visibility of the planet.

Global advertising, far from being satisfied with the classic poster or with breaks between TV or radio programmes, now requires the imposition of its 'environment' on a mass of TV viewers who have in the interim become tele-actors and tele-consumers.

To come back again to the Internet, a number of towns forgotten by tourists vaunt the merits of their regions there. Alpine hotels show off their fine vistas on the screen, while proponents of **land art** are preparing to equip their works with multiple Web cameras. You can also travel vicariously: you can tour America, visit Hong Kong, and even view an Antarctic station in its polar darkness . . .

In spite of its poor optical quality, 'live transmission' has become a promotional tool directing anyone and everyone's gaze to some privileged vantage points.

Happening is no longer a coming to pass; it is merely a passing away. Electronic optics is becoming the 'search engine' of a now globalized fore-sight.

If, in the past, with the telescope, it was simply a matter of observing something unexpected looming up over the horizon, it is now a question of seeing what is happening at the other end of the world, on the hidden side of the planet. Thus, without the aid of the 'artificial horizon' of multi-media, there is no possible way of negotiating the electronic ether of globalization.

The Earth, **that phantom limb**, no longer extends *as far as the eye can see*; it presents all aspects of itself for inspection in the strange little window. The sudden multiplication of 'points of view' merely heralds the latest globalization: the globalization of the gaze, of the single eye of the **cyclops** who governs the cave, that 'black box' which increasingly poorly conceals the great culminating moment of history, a history fallen victim to the syndrome of total accomplishment.

CHAPTER 3

On 20 January 1997, Bill Clinton reasserted in his inaugural address that in the last hundred years the 'promise of
America exploded onto the world stage to make this the
American Century'. He further stated that 'we will redeem
the promise of America in the twenty-first century', with
the USA standing at the head of a whole world of democracies.[1] Yet, in the same address, the president also spoke of
a run-down American model, a fractured, broken-down
democracy, heading, if they were not careful, for a major
political catastrophe.

What is it to be, then? An Americanization of the
world or the disorders of a pseudo-third-worldism extending to assume planetary proportions? And what is an
American century anyway? And what, we may even ask, is
America?

---

1 White House, Office of the Press Secretary, press release 20
January 1997, 12.05 pm EST.

To this latter question, Ray D. Bradbury was fond of replying, 'America is Rembrandt and Walt Disney.' Yet, when Bill Gates (the 'get wired' man) recently wanted to spend some of the pennies he'd been putting aside, he bought not a Rembrandt, but the manuscript of Leonardo da Vinci's *Codex Leicester*. Perhaps because the United States is, in the end, more Italian than Dutch, German, Russian, Hispanic or even WASP. Because, as everyone knows, America was discovered towards the end of the Quattrocento by the Florentine navigator Amerigo Vespucci and the Genoese Christopher Columbus, at a time when other Italians, such as the Genoese Leon Battista Alberti, were introducing the West to *perspectival vision*.

Now, the 'ever-changing skyline' of the historic rush towards the American west is the line of the horizon, the *vanishing point* of the Italian Renaissance, in the strictest sense of the term '*per-spectiva*', which means *seeing through*. The true hero of the American utopia is neither the cowboy nor the soldier, but the pioneer, the pathfinder, the person who 'takes his body to where his eyes have been'.[2]

Before eating up space 'with a voracity unique in the history of human migrations', the pioneer eats it up with his eyes – in America *everything begins and ends with covetousness of the eyes*.

In 1894 the historian Frederick J. Turner wrote:

American social development has been continually beginning over again on the frontier. This perennial

---

2 The expression was coined by Gaston Rébuffat, one of the inventors of 'aid' or 'sixth-class climbing'.

rebirth, this fluidity of American life, this expansion westward with its new opportunities, its continuous touch with the simplicity of primitive society, furnish the forces dominating American character. . . . *The frontier is the line of most rapid and effective Americanization.* The wilderness masters the colonist.[3]

Even today, we old European continentals find it difficult to imagine a state *at peace* which would deny any constant strategic value to its geographical localization, a nation that would merely be a series of virtual trajectories, heading off at great speed towards an unpopulated horizon.

From the beginning, the dimensions of the American state were unstable because they were more astronomical than political. It is because the Earth is round that the European flotilla discovered the New World on the course which led west to Japan and China.

It is again because of the roundness of the planet that the 'ever-changing skyline' of the pioneers can never be reached, that it slips away and endlessly recedes as they approach it. . . . It is merely a delusion, an evanescent optical illusion – not so much an appearance as a *transappearance*.

Everywhere and nowhere, here and elsewhere, neither inside nor outside, the United States represents something

---

3 Frederick Jackson Turner, *The Frontier in American History*, Holt, Rinehart and Winston, New York, 1964, pp. 2–4. The chapter in question was actually read at a meeting of the American Historical Association in Chicago on 12 July 1893. (Trans.)

which had until then no name, a 'beyond' of the ancient colony, an offshore nation. America bears no real relation to the old diaspora or migration of the nomad of former times, who, while advancing rapidly across the treeless plain, frequently turned around to familiarize himself with the lie of the land by which he might return. It is the country of no going back, the land of the one-way ticket – the fateful amalgam of endless racing and the ideas of freedom, progress and modernity.

In conclusion to his famous analysis, Turner was, however, forced to acknowledge: 'Four centuries from the discovery of America . . . the frontier has gone, and with its going has closed the first period of American history.'[4]

The futurist *mise-en-perspective* of the history of the United States seemed to be completed, seemed halted at the outer limit of the continent, on the horizon of the Pacific.

On the eve of this 'American century' of which Bill Clinton spoke in his inaugural address, the United States was, then, still hungry – not so much for territories as for trajectories; hungry to deploy its compulsive desire for movement, hungry to carry on moving so as to carry on being American.

The other day, someone asked Francis Ford Coppola why bad American cinema continued, in spite of everything, to be the stuff of dreams the world over. 'It isn't the films which are the stuff of dreams; it's America, which has become a kind of huge Hollywood,' retorted the Italian-American director.

---

4 Ibid., p. 38.

There are films you are tempted to walk into because you believe they are three-dimensional.

In sending their reporters to the four corners of the Earth, the Lumière brothers had already shown, even at the end of the nineteenth century, that the cinematograph was a substitute for human vision which not only flouted **time** (thanks to the illusion known as persistence of vision), but also flouted the distances and dimensions of real **space**. The cinema was, in fact, a **new energy**, capable of carrying your gaze to other places, even if you yourself did not move.

'One must first speak to the eyes,' said Bonaparte. One can imagine the mileage the America of *perspectiva* – for which 'to halt is to die' – would be able to draw from this technique of *fake movement*, at the very point when the 'ever-changing skyline', which was the engine of its pseudo-democracy, had just come to a juddering halt.

As President William McKinley declared at the beginning of his term of office, the American people did not want 'to go back to the past'.

There would be no resisting the obvious solution: exchanging one lie for another, one illusion for another, one engine for another. And why not?

Since there was no longer a horizon towards which to rush, they would invent fake ones – *substitute horizons*.

The American people would be satisfied. It would not be going back into the past. It would carry on moving towards a 'beyond'.

McKinley also declared that if America elected him, it did so because it was happy to become an industrial nation.

The 'second part of American history' begins not only in the east of the continent, in the mechanical factories of Detroit where production-line working came into operation at the Ford plant around 1914, but also in the west, when, in 1903, a certain Mr Wilcox registered a development of 700 inhabitants in the state of California, which Mrs Wilcox immediately named Hollywood because, as she remarked, holly brings good luck.

It was to be in this outlying suburb of Los Angeles that the American nation was to pursue, 'by other means', its endless race, its journey of no return. With westerns, trail movies, road movies, burlesques, musicals and its most recent productions, such as the *Speed* series,[5] it created a cinema of acceleration, capable of restoring the highest velocity to an 'authentic Americanization'.

Though, at the time, American cinema could not be nationalized, as Soviet cinema was, Hollywood nonetheless lived under close political and ideological surveillance. From Will Hays, the czar of censorship, in the twenties, through the years of William Randolph Hearst's all-powerful press influence and pressure from the upper echelons of the police forces, influential army chiefs, civil and religious leagues, etc., right up to the sinister 1950s, the dark years of McCarthyism.

When, in 1936, Blaise Cendrars managed, not without difficulty, to get into the fortress-studios of American industrial cinema, he sensed there, as in the rest of the country, an air of *mystification*. 'What a good joke!' he

---

5 The US films *Speed* (1994) and *Speed 2* (1997) were directed by Jan de Bont.

wrote. 'But who are they trying to fool here, in this democracy – who but the sovereign people?'

If we believe Turner's analysis, when he speaks of that 'frontier effect' which 'is productive of individualism', and when he argues that 'complex society is precipitated by the wilderness into a kind of primitive organization based on the family [on survivor groups?]. The tendency is anti-social' – then, industrial cinema, by upping its *false frontier effects* to the point of overdose, must inevitably generate social collapse and the generalized political debacle we find at this 'American century'-end.

What began with the grand-scale Hollywood of the 1920s was, in fact, the post-industrial era, the catastrophe of the de-realization of the world. For the leaders of the time the push west was now merely some vague 'cowboy movie', a *trompe-l'oeil* frontier; however, very real migrants, deceived by this optical illusion, still continued to charge towards the Pacific in droves.

Things came to such a pass, indeed, that in the early 1930s California had to cut itself off from the rest of the Union to avoid being submerged by the tide of humanity. It was ringed by the 'blockade', with three divisions of police officers patrolling the frontiers (which had now become internal frontiers) of Oregon, Arizona and Montana. And we should not forget also the mass raids on Mexicans – who were, it was felt, 'taking the bread from the mouths of jobless Americans' – and their brutal deportation. Indigents, tramps, people of colour, lone women, abandoned children, the sick and the infected were pushed back, or pitilessly interned in camps in the desert, health criteria here becoming mingled with social and racial prejudices.

It was a grandiose age in which, after the Wall Street crash in 1929, fifty per cent of the American population lived in near-poverty conditions, forty per cent had only a minimum of sanitary provision, and there were between 18 and 28 million unemployed. Clearly the United States was going through a period of 'growing pains', but on this occasion it was also prepared to drag down a planet which had grown too small for it.

Government by technocrats was soon to follow, in the form of the New Deal with Franklin Delano Roosevelt, who was dubbed the 'New Moses', because he 'led his people out of the desert of poverty . . .'. Before leading them into a *total war* in January 1943 at Casablanca.

'People who don't like television don't like America!' claimed Berlusconi during a memorable election campaign in the Italian style. In the past one might have said the same of those who did not like cinema and today one could say it of people who don't like the Internet or the future information superhighways – those who do not favour *blind* adherence to the ravings of the metaphysicians of techno-culture.

'Admittedly,' says one of those west coast gurus, 'we shall abandon part of the population to their fate when we enter the cyber age, but *techno is our destiny*, the freedom high-tech machines give us is the freedom to be able to say "yes" to their potential.'

The question which now arises is whether we have the freedom to say 'no' to the 'promise' of a yet more 'American century' which lies before us, 'no' to the nihilistic discourse which the America of *perspectiva* and trans-appearance has been endlessly trotting out for 600 years . . . 'Cyber is a new continent, cyber is an additional reality, cyber must reflect the society of individuals, cyber is universal, it has no authorities, no head, etc.'[6]

Meanwhile, Bill Gates was quite happy to put his *Codex* on show at the Musée du Luxembourg in Paris. Among da Vinci's famous 'futuritions', we find a description of the end of the world, its disappearance beneath water. Beneath water or waves perhaps . . . Maybe the old Italian master was not far wrong.

---

6 From comments made at the Cannes *Salon du Milia* 1996–7, by, among others, John Perry Barlow, vice-chair of the Electronic Frontier Foundation.

CHAPTER 4

After Dolly, the predestined sheep, will there soon be human clones? And why not, indeed, since it will be possible before the end of the twentieth century to produce them? Even now, hundreds of men and women are requesting *exact copies* of themselves or *duplicates* of one of their dear departed from the famous Dr Wilmut.

We might say that, for a section of today's public, human cloning is becoming as simple an operation as having one's portrait taken by a photographer in the nineteenth century. Or, since 1895, buying a ticket to see the Lumière brothers' baby guzzling its food up on a screen.[1]

As the century of unbounded curiosity, covetous looking and the de-regulation of the gaze, the twentieth has not

---

1 Louis Lumière had used a portable camera – it weighed barely twelve pounds and was patented on 13 February 1895 – as an amateur photographer, particularly to film his friends and relations. His stated ambition was to *reproduce life*.

been the century of the 'image', as is often claimed, but of optics – and, in particular, of the *optical illusion*.

Since pre-1914 days, the imperatives of propaganda (of advertising) and, subsequently, during the long period of Cold War and nuclear deterrence, security and intelligence needs have gradually drawn us into an intolerable situation in which industrial optics have run wildly out of control.

This has produced the new opto-electronic arsenal, which ranges from remote medical detection devices, probing our 'hearts and loins' in real time, to global remote surveillance (from the street-corner camera to the whole panoply of orbital satellites), with the promised emergence of the cyber-circus still to come.

'The cinema involves putting the eye into uniform,' claimed Kafka.[2] What are we to say, then, of this *dictatorship* exerted for more than half a century by optical hardware which has become omniscient and omnipresent and which, like any totalitarian regime, encourages us to forget we are individuated beings?

If, in terms of current laws, which are supposed to protect individual liberties, we are in fact the owners of our bodies – and *also of the images of those bodies* – our prolific audiovisual environment has long since induced us to cease having any concern for those multiple appearances of ourselves which unknown general staffs – of the military and the police, but also the medical, financial, political, industrial and advertising establishments – steal, misappropriate, explore and manipulate without our knowing it, engaged

---

2 Gustav Janouch, *Conversations with Kafka*, trans. Goronwy Rees, André Deutsch, London, 1968, p. 160.

as they are in secretly fighting over our *optical clones*, our modern mortal remains; to turn them, in the short term, into unconscious actors in their virtual worlds, their nomadic games.

Science-fiction, socio-fiction, political fiction . . . role-playing games, parallel strategies, the divergent and scattered elements of a future cyberspace in which, naturally, 'there is no need to move about in a body like the one you possess in physical reality. . . . Your conditioned notion of a unique and immutable body will give way to a far more liberated notion of "*body*" *as something quite disposable.* . . .'[3]

After the disclosure in March 1996 of the 'mad cow' affair, followed closely by transgenic foodstuffs and animal cloning, the huge marketing operation launched by the 'food power' multinationals is likely, then, to find an audience which, if not informed, is already half-converted. The public will be ready finally to accept that, in the years of global crisis which apparently lie before us, and in a physical world entirely doomed to a joyful *Lust am Untergang*, the evolution of the human species may depend more and more blindly on the expeditious procedures of animal experimentation.

This had long seemed to be presaged in the practice of vivisection, the dissection of living creatures, or rather, as Antonin Artaud put it, creatures *condemned to die alive*.

*

---

3 Howard Rheingold, *Virtual Reality*, Secker and Warburg, London, 1991, p. 191. Rheingold is citing a paper by Walser and Gullichsen.

An old Japanese friend recently confided to me: 'I can't forgive the Americans for the fact that Hiroshima wasn't an act of war, but an experiment.'

The fear today must be that, after the end of East–West nuclear deterrence and the resounding failure of the social experimentation of the early part of the twentieth century, the global economic warfare which has descended on our planet may in turn become experimental and, most significantly, bio-experimental.

Dolly is not, then, an innovation, or even an event. She is a clone in the full sense of the term, a slip or cutting (*klon*) in the strict sense. Before having a future, she has, as the saying goes, 'a past'. It is this which should worry us, this fraught past of our not so much industrial as military-industrial society, in which scientific futurology and crime – all crime – have been closely associated and have progressed together, carrying each other forward.

'There are perhaps just wars, but there are no innocent armies', or so the saying goes. From now on, it is the same with science as it is with war: there is no longer any really innocent science.

If we have long claimed that there existed somewhere a 'tribunal of history', it was doubtless because our history was rather disreputable. We are currently creating a kind of *experimental judicial system* on an international scale which has been given the task of reassuring us, by managing, after a fashion, in public relations terms the ravages and excesses of an *experimental science* which has itself fallen into rather ill repute, and of restoring a semblance of conscience to an applied science which has begun to carry on like an economic 'bad boy' . . .

With the support of the work of these *special tribunals* of a new kind, made up in disparate fashion from scientific and technical experts, a few rare 'moral' personalities and, most recently, representatives of the big corporations, we should not doubt that a case could soon be made for human cloning, and that it could be made legal in the eyes of credulous or profit-hungry populations.

Among these famous *committees* of '*the great and the good*' there are some who are already arguing the benefits of the bio-medical applications of human cloning. But with a little more audacity, could not these spokespeople for scientific futurology soon present it as a possible *repair technique* on an industrial scale, or even advocate the formation of a new sub-proletariat which could be exploited in the event of a great nuclear catastrophe (which is still possible) or genocide?

Yet would such *repair* have what we still by common consent call an *ethical value*? Would it even bear any relation to article 1 of the old Hippocratic oath, the '*primum non nocere*'? Or would it in the end be anything other than *death killing death*, a disguised cruelty?

At the very moment Unesco is granting the ruins of Hiroshima and Auschwitz (those two fields of experimentation) 'historic monument' status, shall we have to admit, after the horrors of war, the errors and errings of a dubious peace?

And can we really contemplate in the near future the industrial breeding and all-out commercialization of human clones, destined, like animals, for *a living death* behind the barbed-wire fences of some experimental farm in the depths of some prohibited area because at least there we wouldn't be able to see these fellows of ours or hear their cries?

Or will these sophisticated procedures merely be transitory? Will they not soon seem too burdensome to their investors and will we not return to the old military and carceral methods in which the soldier (or the condemned man) is no longer treated as an individual, but becomes once again, in Clausewitzian fashion, 'a resource to be mined like any other', *a disposable product . . .?* After the disappearance of the old national armies, to be replaced by the specialists of the new scientific warfare, this would indeed seem a logical step.

Why shouldn't it happen – in an age when the British have refound a vocation as slave-traders and are chartering a prison-ship, a hulk with its containers full of legally prohibited human merchandise; and when ever more radical treatment is being inflicted on migrant populations, those deportees of another age in this post-military-industrial world where triumphalism has grown rare?

A physical world which now offers the spectacle of a routed army – a great headlong flight, with its general staffs of decision-makers vanishing into thin air and yet continuing to issue irresponsible orders and directives no one follows.

With pseudo-individualism, liberal hedonism being nothing more than an 'every man for himself', the mad stampede generated by a general abandonment in which the level of exactions increases and inhibitions explode.

This *tabula rasa* is an ideal situation, a prime opportunity for a scientific futurology which declares itself resolutely schizophrenic and advocates the complete virtualization of living matter, 'humanity being what remains when you have taken from human beings all that can be touched and all that can be seen'.[4]

After the collapse of the hope of any spiritual survival, the great regression of living matter has, then, begun, with the manifest refusal of our age to generate the succeeding ones, and the absolute reversal of the accepted logic of the evolution of species, with the most accomplished link in the chain (the human being?) re-situating itself on its own initiative not far from the very first cell – the point at which the first glimmers of terrestrial life seemingly appeared . . .

With the new *super-conservatism of living matter* outside the 'natural channels' that has insidiously developed within cultures and mentalities during this extraordinary period, this half-century of nuclear deterrence in which we have effectively become temporarily reprieved hostages, populations of living-dead.

From the virtual survival of cryogenics to the vogue for cocooning and the Near Death Experience movement of Dr Moody, to the multiplication of eschatological or pseudo-scientific and technological sects. To the feats of virtual transplants and nano-machines, to *in vitro* and *in vivo* bio-cultures, already applying to the human organism the standard switching of parts which applies in the mechanical world, to the interchangeability of new transhuman beings and, lastly, to suppressing once and for all the pain of living since, by a possible substitutability of cloned bodies, human beings

---

4 Remarks made in March 1997 by a French geneticist and Nobel laureate who sits on an ethics committee.

could still cherish *the hope of surviving themselves while at the same time having ceased to exist.*

It's a bit like the baby who, in the photographic print or the Lumière brothers' film, has gone on guzzling his food just as hungrily since the beginning of the twentieth century, even though he long ago died of old age.

CHAPTER 5

'The war years do not seem like real years. . . . They were a nightmare in which reality stopped,' wrote Agatha Christie not so very long ago.[1]

Today, one feels it no longer takes a war to kill the reality of the world.

Crashes, derailments, explosions, destruction, pollution, the greenhouse effect, acid rain . . . Minamata, Chernobyl, Seveso, etc. In those days of deterrence we eventually got used, after a fashion, to our new nightmare and, thanks among other things to live TV, the long death throes of the planet assumed the familiar guise of one series of scoops among others. Thus, having reached a high degree of '*soft*' *stupor*, we simply contented ourselves with ticking off the events, with enumerating the unfortunate victims of our scientific reverses, our technical and industrial mistakes.

---

1 Agatha Christie, *An Autobiography*, Fontana, London, 1977, p. 525.

But we had seen nothing yet, and where the de-realization of the physical world was concerned, we were soon going to pass on to the next stage. Up till then we had in fact stubbornly refused to concern ourselves with the unparalleled scope of the more perverse harm and more personal troubles caused, not by the spectacular failures of our technical innovations, but by their very performances, their record-breaking feats – the tremendous technological victories won in this critical period in the fields of communications and representation.

It has been claimed that *psychoanalysis does not resolve problems, but merely displaces them* . . . We might say the same of technical and industrial progress.

Even as our famous 'Gutenberg galaxy' was claiming to put reading within everyone's grasp, the reader will note that, at the same time, it mass-produced populations of *deaf-mutes*.

Industrial typography, by spreading the habit of solitary – and hence silent – reading, was gradually to deprive the peoples of that use of speech and hearing which had previously been involved in the (public, polyphonic) reading aloud made necessary by the relative scarcity of manuscripts.

Thus printing forced a degree of impoverishment upon language, which lost not only its *social relief* (primordial eloquence), but also its *spatial relief* (its emphases, its prosody). This was a popular poetics which was not long in withering away, then dying, literally for want of breath, before lapsing into academicism and the unambiguous language of all propaganda, of all advertising.

If we go on drawing up the list of the sensory deprivations we owe to the technological and industrial wastage of our perceptual capacities, we can cite, according to preference, the consenting victims of electricity, those of the photographic snapshot and those of the optical illusion of cinema – these various items of representational equipment which have swelled the ranks of the partially sighted and of those whom Walter Benjamin dubbed *the image illiterates*.

Even in his day, Jean Rostand reckoned that radio 'had not perhaps made us more foolish, but that it had made foolishness noisier'. It was to become deafening with the 'Walkman' and blinding with television and 'that intensification of detail and colour, that bombardment of images which have now replaced words', as Ray Bradbury observed.

'The masses are rushing, running, charging through the age. They think they are advancing, but they are simply running on the spot and falling into the void, that is all,' observed Kafka.

Motion sickness – known technically as 'kinetosis', a condition which makes us part-time members of the disabled community, traveller-voyeurs – was the logical forerunner of *instant transmission sickness*, with the rapid emergence of the 'Net junkies', 'Webaholics' and other forms of cyberpunk struck down with IAD (Internet Addiction Disorder), their memories turned into junkshops – great dumps of images of all kinds and origins, used and shop-soiled symbols, piled up any old how.

While the youngest children, with their noses stuck to the screen from infants' school onwards, are already going down with hyperactivity disorders due to a brain dysfunction which produces erratic activity, serious attention deficits and uncontrollable impulsive acts.

And, with access to the information superhighways set to become more commonplace, an increase in the number of armchair travellers – those distant offshoots of the silent reader – is yet to come. They alone will suffer the full range of communication disturbances acquired over the recent centuries of technology.

In this field *progress* acts like a forensic scientist on us, violating each bodily orifice that is to be autopsied, as a prelude to the brutal incursions that are to follow. It does not simply *affect* individuals, it *penetrates* them. It heaps up, accumulates and condenses in each of us the full range of (visual, social, psycho-motor, affective, intellectual, sexual, etc.) detrital disorders which it has taken on with each innovation, each with their full complement of specific injuries.

Without even suspecting it, we have become the heirs and descendants of some fearsome antecedents, the prisoners of hereditary defects transmitted now not through the genes, sperm or blood, but through *an unutterable technical contamination.*

By virtue of this loss of 'behavioural freedom', all criticism of technology has just about disappeared and we have slid unconsciously from pure technology to techno-culture and, lastly, to the dogmatism of a *totalitarian techno-cult* in which everyone is caught in the trap not of a society and its moral, social or cultural laws and prohibitions, but of what these centuries of progress have made of us and *of our own bodies.*

Those disabled in war or injured in serious road or work accidents, victims of terrorism and people who have lost arms, legs, their mobility, sight, speech or virility are all afflicted at the same time by a forgetting, a paramnesia.

On the one hand, they more or less consciously repress

the unbearable images of the accident which violently deprived them of their able-bodied state; on the other hand, new visions force themselves upon their minds, in sleep or in half-sleep, as a compensation for the motor and sensory privations that now afflict them. In weightless worlds, those who can no longer walk find themselves back on their feet, moving at supernatural speeds. Those who can no longer embrace hug each other for all they are worth, those who can no longer see the light now devour it with eyes filled with wonder. We should not doubt that it is the same with our *technological autotomy* with those *reflex self-mutilations*, whose true causes and circumstances we have long tried to put out of our minds.

As we are gradually deprived of the use of our natural receptor organs, our sensuality, we are obsessed, like the invalid, by a kind of cosmic lack of proper 'measure', by the phantasmatic pursuit of different worlds and modes in which the old 'animal body' would be out of place, in which we would achieve total symbiosis between technology and the human.

'A conglomerate of scanner eyes, nose spasms, wandering tongues, techno-branchiae, cyber ears, sexes without secretions and other organs without bodies. . . .' Those individuals described by a literature which is, says the Canadian Kroker, 'merely an imposture attempting to evade the certainty of death. It is no accident that *cybernetic eternity* is one of the recurrent themes in a discourse in which the physical world dissolves and the cosmos finds itself planted squarely in the computer.'[2]

---

2 Personal communication from Arthur Kroker to Paul Virilio.
  (Trans.)

But let us listen also to Dr Touzeau,[3] who is familiar with other extreme situations:

> By behaviour equivalent to suicide attempts, such as anorexia, mutism, drug abuse and also risk behaviours (excessive speed, riding motorcycles without crash-helmets, etc.), individuals believe they can overcome their own impotence. The backdrop to these violent confrontations with limits is the classic phantasy of being at last able to dominate one's destiny – the phantasy, in short, of *total accomplishment.*

Since the 'Bob Dent affair' of 26 September 1996, when the Australian became the first man to decide to schedule his *computer-aided suicide,* we know that mere tapping on a keyboard can become a risk-behaviour.

Far from arousing compassion, the collective self-immolation of the members of the Heaven's Gate cybersect, announced on the Internet several weeks before the fateful date of 25 March 1997, has been taken as a personal affront by the unquestioning multi-media enthusiasts.

How, they said, could technically sophisticated people, often recruited from American college campuses, have reached such a degree of credulity, such infantilism, as led some of them to have themselves castrated, as though they permanently rejected their manhood, their adulthood?

---

3 The author, with C. Jaquot, of *Traitements de substitution pour les usagers de drogues,* Arnette, Paris, 1998. (Trans.)

This was a question which already troubled Witold Gombrowicz: 'Immaturity is the most effective term to define our contemporaries. . . . An immature state which a *culture that has become inorganic* creates and releases within us.'

Might not the acknowledged disturbance of the maturation process, with its intellectual, sexual, affective and psycho-motor disorders, and the immaturity of individuals who remain arrested in childhood, be the logical outcome and final manifestation of technological defects which have become hereditary?

When cosmonauts floating in their interstellar dustbins cry out to the camera that 'the dream is alive!', why shouldn't Internauts take themselves for cosmonauts? Why would they not, like overgrown fairy-tale children, cross the space between the real and the figurative, reaching as far as the interface with a virtual paradise? Why would they not believe that the extra-terrestrial light of the Hale-Bopp comet is the light that lights up an emergency exit from the physical world? In their luxurious residence of Rancho Santa Fe, the thirty-nine members of the Heaven's Gate cybersect left only their decomposed remains, those bodies they had long since got out of the habit of using.

Chapter 6

'Larry Flynt is still in the street, the fundamentalists are screwed.' This was the *Libération* headline which announced, in that newspaper's own inimitable style, the conclusion of the trial which had pitted the extreme-right French fundamentalist AGRIF organization against Columbia Tristar Film France. But let us recall the facts.

On 17 February 1997 in Paris it was not easy to avoid the posters for a Milos Forman film devoted to the exploits of Larry Flynt, an obscure gangster type who had become the king of the pornographic press in the Reagan years; it was difficult to escape the omnipresent image of a kind of crucified figure hanging from the G-string of a tiny woman.

On 18 February the deputy public prosecutor for the Paris region, taking his lead from an American ruling, expressed an opinion in favour of removing these posters *on grounds of not obstructing the public highway.*

The next day, judge Yves Breillat, retreating perhaps from a decision which might set a precedent, launched into a 'scholarly iconographic analysis' and in the end persuaded the court not to follow the prosecutor's recommendation: the film posters were not to be withdrawn.

A prosecutor pleading infringement of liberties, a judge dismissing the case in the name of specious aesthetic convictions – this banal affair of indirect advertising had at least the merit of revealing once again the shortcomings of a magistracy which is trying as best it can to cope with the progressive disappearance of its traditional reference points. Since, at the time, no blockage had occurred around the posters in question, one might in fact wonder what the public prosecutor could possibly mean by 'obstructing the public highway', unless one were, in fact, to update his argument.

Since the posting of advertisements is designed to arrest the gaze and capture attention, it is regarded as dangerous for precisely these reasons and is duly regulated along fast roads and on the main highways.

The law of 1979 in France even accepts the notion of 'visual pollution', which may be caused by not only the positioning, but also the lighting, and the density and proliferation of advertising material outside large conurbations.

Was it our prosecutor's ambition to see these restrictive measures extended to the cityscape? Might what is illicit in the countryside also become so in the town?

Why not? – when we know that, by their own admission, American advertisers are now setting about what they term a *new world ecology*, in which it will be possible within a few hours to inundate all the great cities of the planet with thousands of copies of a single poster – which would force every city-dweller on the planet, against their will, to view something now no longer offered for their contemplation, but *imposed upon their gaze.*

By proceeding against the poster for Milos Forman's film not merely for its blasphemous content or its obscenity, but also for its infringement of essential freedoms, the public prosecutor was projecting us into a completely opposite scenario: was not the blustering Larry Flynt, the Christ of porn, the martyr of freedom of expression, the defender of non-conformism, actually the symbolic instrument of an enterprise with totalitarian aims?

Indeed, where the – direct and indirect – advertising campaign surrounding Flynt's exploits is concerned, another pressing question arises: can the world of the night be over-exposed and dragged into the light without ceasing to be itself? *Can what was* marginal *yesterday become* mainstream *with impunity*?

As we see once again with the rather lame verdict arrived at on 19 February 1997, one of the major difficulties encountered by the porn market is that it is not really accepted in the public sphere. Like prostitution, it has difficulty escaping 'the private world of indecency' and finding a proper legal footing in public spaces and on our highways and byways, which, as everyone knows, are among the last legal refuges of a certain morality and its prohibitions (on drugs, alcohol, sex, etc.).

Unless pornography achieves a conflation with another form of international traffic – the traffic in culture.

This was, we may note, the option chosen by judge Breillat. The real issue in the Larry Flynt affair was this fusion/confusion of pornography with that *freedom of expression* generally accorded to cultural activities.

One frequently hears it proclaimed that 'Art cannot be

immoral', whereas what ought to be said is that *it cannot be illegal.*

In losing any sacred character, it long since entered the baneful Goethean triangle of 'war, commerce and piracy, the three in one, inseparable' (Faust II).[1]

For a long time now, too, the 'art lover' has been transformed into a silent witness wandering through galleries and museums which with total impunity contain the illicit products of wartime plunder, ethnic massacres and other criminal acts (tomb-raiding, dismantling of religious buildings, etc.).

Anglo-Saxon free-market economics merely confirms this state of affairs when it advocates non-discrimination in trade and wishes to include culture in the 'service category' and as one of the many spin-off products offered to consumers by the multinationals (games, films, CDs, travel, etc.).

With the *invisible trade* in services succeeding, and even opposing, the *visible trade* in goods, advertisers assert that they are no longer there simply to sell objects, but to create new forms of behaviour and to serve as counterweights to industrialist pressure.

In 1993, at the time of the General Agreement on Tariffs and Trade (GATT) negotiations, this type of immaterial operation already accounted for more than sixty per cent of the gross national product (GNP) of the industrialized countries and represented thirty-five per cent of international transactions. And when you see professionals

---

1 'Krieg, Handel und Piraterie/Dreieinig sind sie, nicht zu trennen' (Act 5, Scene 2, lines 1187–8).

like those in the Disney Corporation shedding the Puritanism appropriate to a disappearing family market and going in for hyper-violence on the ABC channel, and sex, with, among other things, 'Gay days' at Disneyland and Disneyworld, you can better discern the objectives of a porn market which is not without its by-products either. By merging, and becoming confused, with culture it might finally escape the last legal restrictions and would also profit from non-discrimination with regard to 'services' . . .

What Benetton and other advertisers had attempted on commercial pretexts, the national museums and art galleries were to achieve *culturally*.[2]

It was noted in 1996 in Paris that the major Cézanne exhibition did not achieve the expected success (600,000 visitors), in spite of the praiseworthy efforts of the organizers. Conversely, at the same time the public rushed to the Georges Pompidou Centre to see the little exhibition 'Masculin/Féminin' with its rows of genital organs and its pornographic graffiti, which were clearly more exciting than Cézanne's austere bathers.

The Musée d'Orsay having no doubt decided to revive its financial fortunes, that November one could not avoid

---

2 The formation of the sex–culture–advertising enterprise did not take place yesterday, as Magritte noted. 'What Surrealism means officially: an advertising enterprise carried on with sufficient savoir-faire and conformism to have as much success as other enterprises. . . . Thus the "surrealist woman" was an invention as stupid as the "pin-up girl" which is now replacing her.' Cited by Georges Roque, *Ceci n'est pas une Magritte*, Flammarion, Paris, 1983.

its posters reproducing part of Gustave Courbet's painting entitled *The Origin of the World*.[3] The part in question was in fact a quasi-photographic close-up of the pubic region of a reclining woman with her thighs parted.

The cultural pretext did its job perfectly in this case: no one lodged a complaint and no public prosecutor was found to request the withdrawal of this poster, which was far more pornographic than the one for the Milos Forman film.

The crowd of those people who 'think of sex every seventy seconds' – as certain British advertisers claim – joined with the throng of art-lovers and they all headed off for the Musée d'Orsay to take a closer look between the legs of Courbet's sturdy maiden.

Still in pursuit of a majority market, the Georges Pompidou Centre organized its 'Seven Deadly Sins' exhibition the following year, while the Cartier Foundation offered 'Amours' – significantly, in the plural.

In Barcelona, it was the 'Primavera del Disseny' (the Spring Festival of Design), where 'Some twenty photographers, designers, architects and graphic artists went crazy over sex maliciously or crudely.' Everywhere, from Los Angeles to Hanover, in galleries and museums they stopped *practising dissimulation*.

A literature also emerged, the central aim of which was to convince the general public that our great artists, from Rodin to Delacroix and from Brecht to Bataille, were sexually obsessed and had never feared moral opprobrium.

---

3 1866. Oil on canvas. 46 × 55cm. Private collection. (Trans.)

Not wanting to be left behind, the classical music world also joined in, and the respectable Opéra de Paris staged Rossini's *Italian Girl in Algiers* in a 'hardcore' version in which the 'director revelled in allusions (pairs of inflatable breasts, simulations of rectal penetration, Turkish massages) without, however, daring to become pornographic,' complained a Parisian critic.

This was not the case with Angela Marshall, an American artist who, in a London gallery, sold both her artworks and her body: 'As long as the public hasn't made love, it isn't art!' she explained, indicating her prices.

This slippage which was occurring from the culture market (and even hypermarket)[4] to the pornography market became a cause for concern to the genuine professionals of the night, who saw a large number of their traditional outlets slipping away. To attempt to rectify this situation, a 'Museum of Eroticism' was opened in Pigalle.

Since the game typically consists in taking on, one after the other, the bastions of a certain 'cultural respectability', London's Royal Academy of Art was the next obvious target. That was where an exhibition named 'Sensation' was held in 1997, allegedly to showcase young British artists.

In reality, it was a new 'war machine', designed by the sex–culture–advertising movement, which was present in full there, since the 110 works on display (a portrait of the

---

4 Cf. Bazart, the hypermarket of contemporary art founded in Barcelona in 1994. In this itinerant exhibition and sale, which 'gets back to the spirit of the boutique', *art becomes*, we are told, *'a consumer product like any others, with new stocks coming in all the time'*.

child-murderer Myra Hindley, casts of childlike bodies with mouths replaced by phalluses, etc.) belonged, without exception, to Charles Saatchi, one of Britain's great advertising moguls.

In another unprecedented move, one room in the gallery, in which the most violent and obscene works were grouped, was out of bounds to those under eighteen years of age. This marks the abolition of one of the last differences that still existed between so-called cultural events and any other X-rated show.

In response to the scandal the organizers had been hoping for, the exhibition's curator merely repeated the time-honoured formula: 'Art is never immoral.' Abandoning all modesty, all reserve, is not an immoral attitude, it is a *dangerous attitude*.

It is to forget, it seems, that the word 'obscene' comes from the Latin *obscenus*, which means *ill-omened*, a sign of a fearsome future.

As early as the 1920s, when the great art dealer René Gimpel had the chance to see the works of the German Expressionists in Berlin, he was seized with apprehension and felt no good would come of them. It was not long before he was able to verify, in the Neuengamme concentration camp (where he was to die on 1 January 1945), 'what horrors the human imagination could conceive on the basis of an almost ingenuous idea called love, up to and including the *danse macabre* painted on the wall of the charnel houses'.[5] The reader will have noted that up to this

---

5 Pierre Mac Orlan, *Nuits aux bouges*, Les Éditions de Paris, Paris, 1994.

point the new artists contented themselves with using animal corpses preserved in formalin, confining themselves, where human beings were concerned, to mere anatomical casts.

The line was to be crossed in 1998 with the 'Körperwelten' (Body Worlds) exhibition at the Landesmuseum für Technik und Arbeit in Mannheim. Around 780,000 visitors thronged there to contemplate 200 human corpses presented by a certain Günther von Hagens.

This German anatomist actually invented a process for preserving dead bodies and, most important, *sculpting* them by coating them with plastic.[6] He presented flayed figures, standing like ancient statues, some brandishing their skins like a trophy, others exhibiting their viscera in the manner of Dalí's *Venus de Milo of the Drawers*.

As his sole explanation, Dr von Hagens was content merely to mouth the slogan: 'I am breaking down the last taboos.'

There is a slippage going on here and, as time goes by, one will soon be able to apply the term 'avant-garde artists' not just to the German Expressionists inciting to murder, but to others among their unknown contemporaries, who should have their place in the very particular collections of our century.

Take, for example, Ilse Koch, that romantic blonde who in 1939 alighted upon a shaded valley near Weimar, the

---

6 Dr von Hagens's technique, known as 'plastination', involves replacing water with a curable polymer. It is widely used throughout the world in the teaching of anatomy, pathology, etc. (Trans.)

very spot where Goethe loved to walk and where he had conceived his Mephistopheles, *the universally nay-saying spirit*: 'The work began at once and the camp quite naturally received the name of the forest so dear to the poet – Buchenwald.'[7]

The woman who was subsequently to be nicknamed 'the bitch of Buchenwald' clearly could not have known Dr von Hagens's ingenious procedure, but she had aesthetic aspirations quite similar to his, since she had her unfortunate lovers flayed and from their skins made objects such as lampshades or wallets.

'The artist first contributes his body,' said Paul Valéry.

During the 1960s, the Viennese Actionists had followed this watchword to the letter, since it was their own bodies they used as the medium of their art.

After Hermann Nitsch's 'masses', in which he sacrificed animals 'in a lewd, bloody ritual', the most extreme example of Actionism will surely remain that of Rudolf Schwarzkogler. His death was attributed to the after-effects of the castration he inflicted upon himself during one of his performances, one of his 'actions' which took place with no audience, in a private encounter between the artist and a camera.

These are extreme arts, in the same way as one speaks of 'extreme sports', in which the main object, in particular, is to suffer – *terminal arts*, since they require nothing for their

7 G. Rabinovitch, 'Le chêne de Buchenwald', *Traces*, no. 3, Paris; see also Walter Laqueur, *The Terrible Secret: Suppression of the Truth about Hitler's 'Final Solution'*, Weidenfeld and Nicholson, London, 1980.

fulfilment but a confrontation between a tortured body and an automatic camera.

These visual arts, which Schopenhauer referred to as the suspension of the pain of living, became, in the twentieth century, a precipitation towards pain and death for individuals who have acquired the ill-considered habit of leaving their corpses to scientific voyeurism, and now these others, who give theirs up to the 'art' of Dr von Hagens.

In 1906 *The World*, a New York daily, ran the headline: 'Give Me My Father's Body!' This referred, in fact, to the plea of a young Inuit (Eskimo) boy who had discovered that the skeleton on display in a case in the New York Natural History Museum was that of Quisuk, his own father.

Nine years earlier the father had died, with four of his Eskimo companions, from the ravages of tuberculosis, not long after landing on American soil.

Young Minik, who was then eight years old, had attended the funeral, but this had just been a masquerade organized by scientists from Columbia University's anthropology department, who wished to appropriate the remains and prevent the child from discovering that his father was now part of the museum's collection.[8]

Robert Peary, who was later to reach the North Pole, bears considerable responsibility in this affair, for he regarded the Eskimos as sub-humans, as 'the useful instruments of his Arctic work'.

Our visual arts were neither first, nor alone (far from it), in anticipating the 'cabinet of horrors of the twentieth

---

8 Kenn Harper, *Give Me My Father's Body*, Blacklead Books, Iqaluit, Nunavut, 1986.

century'. The avant-garde of modernity did not fashion itself in the shadow of the art galleries and national museums, but in natural history museums like the one in which the young Inuit was to discover, among the ruins of the civilization of Thule, his father's skeleton transformed into a numbered specimen.

In the classical art museum, the fruits of dubious expeditions were exhibited as though legal exemption had already been granted. In the New York museum we see a troubling updating of these practices of impunity.

Thus the sordid crime of the New York museum, revealed in 1906 by *The World*, was absolved in advance at the moment when the world's press was making the conquest of the North Pole one of the most exciting – scientific, sporting, cultural – objectives of our civilization. A moment when *humanity could stand the strain of waiting no longer:* 'It was a disgrace,' wrote Karl Kraus,

> that *we, the owners of the world, should have let ourselves be deprived of its last little slice.* . . . For the only valuable thing about the North Pole was that it had not been reached. Once it had been reached, it is just a pole from which a flag waves – thus worse than nothing, a crutch of fulfilment and a barrier to imagination. . . . The discovery of the North Pole . . . is an effective extemporization of a past development. [emphasis added][9]

9 'The Discovery of the North Pole', ed. Harry Zohn, *In These Great Times: A Karl Kraus Reader*, Carcanet, Manchester, 1976, p. 50.

And Kraus concluded: '"The greatest man of the century" is the title of the hour; the next hour bestows it upon someone else. . . . People were sated with the North Pole, and never before had they been disillusioned so suddenly and so painfully.'[10]

The international press, less changeable than it seemed, registered the painful completion of the geographical conquest and anticipated, in alarmist despatches, the new major event which might be said to be its direct consequence. That was the coming, five years later, of a first **world** war which, by its very universalism, would become the *first total war* of humanity *against* man thanks to the deployment of a military-industrial arsenal of mass destruction, which was soon to encompass a scientific complex ranging from physics to biology and psychology.[11]

It was merely a question of time, then, for the transfer of the West's *expansionist drives* from the exhausted geography of the terrestrial to the human body – that last, still-unexplored corner of the planet, relatively protected by the last cultural, social and moral prohibitions . . .

And for the solemn celebrations, such as those which attended the end of slavery and the defence of human rights, to become merely sinister masquerades – only poorly concealing the drift, from the 1940s onwards, of a *colonial savoir-faire* towards a world-scale project of an *endocolonial* nature. One has only to look to see this: with the rise of unemployment and cultural integration, the abandonment of the nourishing countryside for the over-populated and

---

10 Ibid., p. 55.
11 Paul Virilio, *Essai sur l'insécurité du territoire*, Stock, Paris, 1976.

unproductive ghettos, and galloping pauperization, our post-industrial world is already the spitting image of the old colonial world, examples of which we find in Africa, Latin America or the Far East.

And we can rest assured that, after the unrestrained exploitation of the living Earth and its *geography*, the exploitation of the *cartography* of the human genome is already well advanced. This is a project which tells us a great deal about a booming industrial techno-biology, whose ambition is to reduce to the state of *specimen* every member of a humanity which has had its day, every human being who, like young Minik's father, might be said no longer precisely to be an individual, no longer *individuum–indivisible*.

As the dominant influence of the nineteenth-century scientistic and positivistic philosophies draws to a close, one can better discern the usefulness of the new *sex–culture–advertising* complex and the predominant promotional role it plays in this 'phenomenon of evil deeds committed on a gigantic scale, which could not be traced to any particularity of wickedness'.[12]

So far as the so-called arts of representation are concerned, the *anonymity* of anatomy beneath the human skin had already showed through in the work of da Vinci, a development later to be confirmed by Rembrandt and later Géricault hovering around the morgues of the great hospitals, and even in the Cubism of Picasso, who painted

---

12 Hannah Arendt, 'Thinking and Moral Considerations: A Lecture', *Social Research*, fall 1970, vol. 38, no. 3, p. 147.

his portraits of women 'the way you dissect a corpse', as Apollinaire remarked.

This banalization of *cold perception* – paradoxically, a privileged feature of the scientific gaze – in fact developed an aesthetics specific to that gaze: a kind of *elementary structuralism* which was to infuse fields as various as the visual arts, literature, industry, design or even the social and economic utopias of the nineteenth and twentieth centuries.[13]

However, when the Viennese Actionists insist upon the private encounter with the camera for their performances, the *watching gaze* has long since ceased to be that of the artist or even the scientist, but belongs to the instruments of technological investigation, to the combined industrialization of perception and information.

Writing of photography, Walter Benjamin incautiously explained: 'It prepares that salutary movement by which man and the surrounding world become alien to each other, opening up a field in which all intimacy yields to the illumination of detail.'

This precisely describes the endocolonization of a world without intimacy which we are seeing – a world which has become alien and obscene, entirely given over to information technologies and the over-exposure of detail.

---

13 'The invisible truth of bodies', seen on the eve of the French Revolution, in works like Jacques Agoty's claiming to illustrate 'the interaction between the scalpel and the engraver's chisel', and closed systems such as Georges Cuvier's law of subordination of the organs and the correlation of forms which inspired Balzac in his studies of social life.

CHAPTER 7

To fight against the ghosts which seemed to be assailing her, a twenty-five-year-old American, June Houston, has just installed fourteen cameras in her house, providing constant surveillance of strategic sites: under the bed, in the basement, outside the front door, etc.

Each of these 'live-cams' is supposed to transmit *sightings* on to a Web site. So the visitors who consult this site become 'ghost watchers'.

A dialogue box allows you to send a message to alert the young woman via the Internet if any kind of 'ectoplasm' should manifest itself.

'It is as though the Internauts were becoming neighbours, witnesses to what is happening to me,' declared June Houston.[1]

With this voyeurism, tele-surveillance takes on a new meaning. It is no longer a question of forearming oneself

---

1 *Le Monde*, 18 November 1997.

against an interloper with criminal intent, but of sharing one's anxieties, one's obsessive fears with a whole network, through over-exposure of a living space.

'I don't want people to come physically into my space. So, until I understood the potential of the Internet, I couldn't get any outside help.'

By this admission, June Houston illustrates the nature of the so-called virtual community and the phantasmic existence of a new type of localness, of social 'tele-localness' which totally revolutionizes the notion of neighbourhood, the temporal and spatial unity of physical cohabitation.

Moreover, some Internet users send the young woman genuine 'surveillance reports', indicating what they believe they have seen in her home. The site is code-named 'Flyvision'.

This anecdote shows strikingly the emergence of a new kind of **tele-vision**, a television which no longer has the task of informing or entertaining the mass of viewers, but of exposing and invading individuals' domestic space, like a new form of lighting, which is capable of revolutionizing the notion of *neighbourhood unit*, or of a building or district.

Thanks to this 'real-time' illumination, the space-time of everyone's apartment becomes potentially connected to all others, the fear of exposing one's private life gives way to the desire to over-expose it to everyone, to the point where, for June Houston, the arrival of 'ghosts', which she so dreads, is merely the pretext for the invasion of her dwelling by the 'virtual community' of furtive Internet inspectors and investigators.

Flyvision – *'vision volante'* – is also *'vision volée'*, stolen vision: a vision from which the blind spots of daily life disappear.

It is, in fact, fair to say that this practice revolutionizes classical local television from top to bottom. It revolutionizes the broadcasting of information programmes by contributing to the total transformation of the *transparency* of sites and spaces of habitation, in the direction of a purely mediatic *trans-appearance* of the real space of living beings.

Now, this paradoxical situation is currently becoming widespread, since the 'globalization of the single market' demands the over-exposure of every activity; it requires the simultaneous creation of competition between companies, societies and even consumers themselves, which now means individuals, not simply certain categories of 'target populations'.

Hence the sudden, untimely emergence of a universal, *comparative advertising*, which has relatively little to do with publicizing a brand or a consumer product of some kind, since the aim is now, through the *commerce of the visible*, to inaugurate a genuine **visual market**, which goes far beyond the promoting of a particular company.

Seen like this, the gigantic concentration of telephone, television and computer communications companies becomes easier to understand – the MCI-WORLD COM merger (the biggest transaction of all time) and the sudden conversion of Westinghouse, which was once an electricity production company and has now moved into the world telecommunications business.

After the *direct lighting* of cities by the magic of electricity in the twentieth century, the companies created by these mergers are pioneering an *indirect lighting* of the world for the twenty-first century.

Thanks to the promises of the magic of electronics,

electro-optic lighting is going to assist in the emergence of the virtual reality of cyberspace. Building the space of the multi-media networks with the aid of tele-technologies surely then requires a new 'optic', a new **global optics**, capable of helping a **panoptical** vision to appear, a vision which is indispensable if the 'market of the visible' is to be established.

The much-vaunted **globalization** requires that we all observe each other and compare ourselves with one another on a continual basis.

Like June Houston, every economic and political system in its turn enters the private life of all the others, forbidding any of them to free themselves for any length of time from this competitive approach.

Hence a recent decision by the European Community to pass legislation on 'comparative advertising', in order to oppose systematic negative advertising campaigns and to ensure the protection of consumers from the verbal violence involved in this type of commercial promotion.[2]

Today, *control of the environment* is very largely supplanting the *social control* of the constitutional state and, to this end, it has to establish a new type of transparency: *the transparency of appearances instantaneously transmitted over a distance* . . . This is the meaning of the commerce of the visible, the very latest form of 'publicity'.

For a multinational company or a society, the aim of acquiring a global dimension requires **all-out** competition, 'all-out' being a term that has fallen into disuse since the end of the Cold War ('all-out' nuclear war, etc.)

---

2 *Le Monde*, 16 September 1997.

Making information resonate globally, which is necessary in the age of the great planetary market, is in many
ways going to resemble the practices and uses of military
intelligence, and also political propaganda and its excesses.

'*He who knows everything fears nothing,*' claimed Joseph
Paul Goebbels not so long ago. From now on, with the
putting into orbit of a new type of panoptical control, *he
who sees everything* – or almost everything – will have nothing more to fear from his immediate competitors.

You will, in fact, understand nothing of the *information
revolution* if you are unable to divine that it ushers in, in
purely cybernetic fashion, the *revolution of generalized snooping*.

How indeed is one to keep watch on the initiatives of
one's competitors at the other end of the planet and obtain
a sample of a product which threatens your own? Since
1991, the French company Pick Up has met such a
demand by creating a network of informers in twenty-five
countries. Its journalists, investigators and consultants of
various kinds – generally natives of the countries concerned – have had the task of maintaining an *all-out
technological vigil*.[3]

And, in fact, some investigation agencies now act like
real private information multinationals, battling over highly
lucrative markets throughout the world.

As examples, we might cite the American Kroll agency,
the British companies Control Risk and DSI, or, in South
Africa, the Executive Outcomes agency.[4]

---

3 *Le Nouvel Observateur*, 10 July 1997.
4 See the article by Laurent Léger, *Paris-Match*, autumn 1997.

These are all variants on an investigation market which is taking on something of the appearance of totalitarian espionage.

After the first bomb, the *atom bomb*, which was capable of using the energy of radioactivity to smash matter, the spectre of a second bomb is looming at the end of this millennium. This is the information bomb, capable of using the interactivity of information to wreck the peace between nations.[5]

'On the Internet, there is a permanent temptation to engage in terrorism, as it is easy to inflict damage with impunity,' declared a one-time hacker who is now a company director,

> and this danger grows with the arrival of new categories of Internet users. The worst are not, as is generally believed, the political activists, but *the unscrupulous little businessmen who will go to any lengths to do down a competitor who gets in their way.*

Their preferred weapons? The new bulk-mailing software, invented by advertising people, which can submerge a particular server in a veritable 'mail-bombing' campaign that enables anyone to become a 'cyber-terrorist' at little risk to themselves.

Once again, then, we see economic warfare advancing under the cover of promoting the greatest freedom of

---

5 'La bombe informatique: entretien de Paul Virilio et Frederick Kittler', *Arte*, 15, 1995.

communication, and in this kind of 'informational' conflict, advertising strategies have to be recast.

In his book, *La Publicité est-elle une arme absolue?*, the
chairman of the Jump agency, Michel Hébert, tries to
demonstrate the need for 'guerrilla business', explaining
that the chain of communication has to be transformed
from top to bottom.[6]

Hence the resistible rise of so-called interactive advertising, which combines audiovisual entertainment with
marketing effectiveness.

In France today, 700,000 households can show their inter-
est in a product presented in a television advert by simply
pressing the OK button on their remote control keypad,
thanks to the 'Open TV' and 'Media Highway' software
(for the TPS and Canal Satellite channels respectively).

This is the consecration on mass TV of a kind of advertising which previously existed only on the Internet.

From *interactive* to *comparative* advertising is only a small
step. *A small step for man, but a giant leap for inhumanity.*

A giant leap towards 'mass snooping', the industrialization of informing.

'Comparisons are misleading', as the old saying goes.
But currently, with the single market's requirement for
global competition, comparison has become a **globalitarian** phenomenon, which requires the full-scale
over-exposure not just of places – as with the remote surveillance of roads – but also of persons, their behaviour,
their actions and innermost reactions.

---

6 'Naissance du business de guérilla', *Le Figaro*, 11 November
1997.

Thus the misleading nature of enforced competition becomes a part of our economic, political and cultural activities.

The multinational enterprise sidelines the weak at their keypads; it sidelines these new 'citizens of the world' as mere consumers of a kind of *parlour game* in which the conditioned reflex wins out over shared reflection. Might is right, but not rational here in a statistical phenomenon of the massification of social behaviour which threatens democracy itself.

As Albert Camus wittily observed, 'When we are all guilty, that will be true democracy!'

After ordinary 'grassing', calumny and slander – not to mention the social ravages of rumour-mongering, free telephone lines for 'informers' and telephone taps on suspects – we are now entering the era of *optical snooping*. This is bringing a general spread of surveillance cameras, not just into the streets, avenues, banks or supermarkets, but also into the home: in the housing estates of the poorer districts and, above all, with the worldwide proliferation of 'live-cams' on the Internet, where you can visit the planet from your armchair thanks to Earthcam, a server which already has 172 cameras sited in twenty-five countries. Or, alternatively, you can have access through Netscape Eye to thousands of on-line cameras angled not just at tourism and business but towards a generalized introspection.

These are emblematic of a universal voyeurism which directs everyone's gaze towards privileged 'points of view', the sudden increase in 'points of view' never being any other than a heralding of the future 'points of sale' of the latest globalization: *the globalization of the gaze of the single eye.*

Active (wave) optics, which revolutionizes the traditional passive (geometric) optics of the era of Galileo's telescope, as though the loss of the horizon of geographical perspective necessitated the establishment of a substitute horizon – the **artificial horizon** of a screen or a monitor capable of permanently displaying the preponderance of the media perspective, the relief of the 'tele-present' event taking precedence over the three dimensions of the volume of the objects or places *here present*.

Hence this proliferation of 'great lights in the sky' – observation or communications satellites – which are preparing to saturate the orbital space of our planet, with the launch of Motorola's Iridium project, of Teledesic and the Alcatel company's Skybridge.

'Faster, smaller, cheaper' – this NASA slogan could shortly become the watchword of globalization itself. But with one nuance, since the *speed* and *smallness* in question would no longer refer to devices designed to conquer extra-terrestrial space, but to our geography at the moment of its sudden temporal compression.

The societies of confinement denounced by Michel Foucault are being succeeded, then, by the societies of control announced by Gilles Deleuze.

Have they not in France just authorized the use of *electronic tagging devices* on prisoners released on parole, **transponders** which enable them to be located at any point, thus avoiding further pressure on already overcrowded prisons?

These inaugural practices – which will undoubtedly be extended in the future to other categories of deviants, to those who do not conform to the norm — are today described as 'humanitarian'.

And what are we to say of the enthusiasm of post-industrial companies for the cellphone which enables them to abolish the distinction between working hours and private life for their employees?

Or the introduction in Britain not simply of 'part-time' but of 'zero-hour' contracts, accompanied by the provision of a mobile phone. When the company needs you, *it calls and you come running*. The reinvention of a domestic servility ultimately on a par with the *electronic incarceration* of offenders in the closed circuit of a police station.

The smaller the world becomes as a result of the relativistic effect of telecommunications, the more violently situations are concertinaed, with the risk of an economic and social **crash** that would merely be the extension of the **visual crash** of this 'market of the visible', in which the *virtual bubble* of the (interconnected) financial markets is never any other than the inevitable consequence of that *visual bubble* of a politics which has become both **panoptical** and **cybernetic**.

June Houston, our paranoid American, is then the unwitting heroine of a game which is merely beginning, a game in which everyone inspects and watches over all the others, looking for a *spectre* which is no longer haunting Europe alone, but the whole world — the world of business and global geopolitics. Furthermore, our unbalanced American friend takes her inspiration from the screens of Wall Street, updating the site report on her home every two or three minutes, thus keeping up the attentiveness of watchers who — like New York's traders — are never really discouraged by anything. All the more so as our attractive American lady posts photos of herself on the site from time to time – **still photos**, of course.

Chapter 8

Following a complaint lodged by a feminist anti-rape collective, a poster extolling the merits of a major chocolate brand was immediately withdrawn, with apologies from the advertising agency.

On the poster in question, you saw the black supermodel Tyra Banks, her body naked and dripping with long patches of white – cream, no doubt. And alongside, in large lettering, were the words '*It's no use saying "no", they hear "yes".*' What alerted the anti-rape defence league was not so much the image of this defiled female body as the commentary accompanying it: a 'no' heard as a 'yes'. *The metaphor of a voice being silenced.*

Yet this typically audiovisual phenomenon is reproduced every day in the mass media, in particular in television. When the control room puts through images of violence, sex and gore, the current affairs reporters are required to comment on them in expurgated language, in order not to offend or deter any category of listeners, any (economic, racial, clinical, sexual, etc.) community, and hence keep the audience figures stable.

With live coverage (either in real time or with a slight delay), this internal contradiction has become very difficult – if not indeed impossible – to manage, since to the technical hitches of yesteryear have now been added the formidable dangers of the instant commentary for reporters who find themselves at the frontiers of the word and the image, permanently caught between a 'soft' (politically correct) language and the 'hard' (visually incorrect) images of 'see-it-now'-style broadcasting.

We also find this dilemma among other professionals – the dilemma of a language which has become embarrassing and embarrassed. For example, when a top dress designer was recently asked why supermodels had replaced actresses and movie stars in the popular press, he simply replied, 'Because they don't speak.' For the international supermodel, the dilemma of audiovisual communication has been resolved by lopping off speech altogether.

We can hardly be surprised, then, at the new *visual* trends of a haute couture which has become Babelish and those fashion shows where, we are told, *designers will do anything* for the international cameras, like the English 'rude boys' who, for a time, took over the old fashion houses such as Dior or Givenchy. One of these is, indeed, the designer of a collection of women's clothing and underclothes which are torn and stained blood-red, the name of which is 'Rape in the Highlands'.

In the early years of the twentieth century, the novelist Paul Morand observed: 'Speed, in slamming two caresses together, turns them into a mortal impact.' Has not rape perhaps become the unacknowledged by-product of a technological emergency that is becoming routinized?

Between July 1962, when American Telephone and Telegraph's Telstar satellite was successfully launched, enabling the first direct television link-up between the USA and Europe to take place, and the generalized switching between multi-media we see today, the world has made a sudden transition from the 'hear-it-now' to the over-exposure of the 'see-it-now'. From now on, whether we like it or not, any interpersonal relationship, any entry into communication, any cognitive procedure involves us unconsciously in that unsanctioned violence of an *optical shock* which has become global. In this way, the revolutionary ethic of a (hard) image perceived in real time will soon lead to a lifting of the *moral prohibitions* which still applied to pornography and obscene acts on the screen. It also explains the size of the market for these things on the Minitel system or the Internet.

There is nothing enticing about our supermodels any more once they been reduced to silence. Their bodies are not just denuded, but *silently* exposed, without saying a word, to laboratory sufferings – from plastic surgery to testosterone.

Let us make no mistake about it, if they are starting a fashion, it is not a fashion in clothing. The supermodels are already mutants ushering in an unprecedented event: *the premature death of any living language.*

The new electronic Babel might be said to be dying not from the plethora of languages, but from their disappearance. And it seems not to be a matter of speaking to one another, writing and thinking, like the North Americans, in a standard pseudo-English, but doing all these things at the same time, more and more quickly.

'Brevity is the soul of e-mail,' Nicholas Negroponte tells internauts in *Being Digital*. And the billionaire George Soros for his part asserts, 'I am capable of reducing the most complex situation *to its simplest expression*.'

Technological acceleration initially brought about a transference from writing to speech – from the letter and the book to the telephone and the radio. Today it is the spoken word which is logically withering away before the instantaneity of the real-time image. With the spread of illiteracy, the era of silent microphones and the mute telephone opens before us. The instruments will not remain unused on account of any technical failings, but for lack of sociability, because we shall shortly have nothing to say to each other, or really the time to say it – and, above all, we shall no longer know how to go about listening to or saying something, just as we already no longer know how to write, in spite of the fax revolution which was allegedly going to give letter-writing a new lease of life.

After the brutal extinction of the host of dialects spoken by tribes and families, and their replacement by the academic language of expanding nations, a language now unlearned and supplanted by the global vocabulary of e-mail, we may now envisage planetary life becoming progressively a story without words, a silent cinema, an authorless novel, comics without speech-bubbles . . .

But also, in the generalized violence of acceleration, we can envisage suffering passing without complaint; horrors going unbewailed, not that there would be anyone to hear the wailing; and anxieties going without a prayer – and without even an analysis.

As Caspar David Friedrich sensed, '*The peoples will no*

longer have a voice. They will no longer be allowed to be aware of themselves, take pride in themselves.'

'Politics is a theatre often played out on a scaffold,' said (more or less) St Thomas More, who learned the lesson to his cost.

The screen has today replaced the scaffold where, according to the author of *Utopia*, the political was killed in the past. In fact, the audiovisual dilemma has become the most certain threat hanging over our old democracies, which are so aptly named '*representative*'. The foremost political art was eloquence, that democratic eloquence which, in return, gathers to it the *voice* of the nation – the popular votes, the popular suffrage.

Our statesmen were men of the forum, the platform and the public meeting. Their speeches might last three or four hours. They were lawyers, publicists, journalists, writers, poets . . .

One may ask oneself today this simple question: how would great historic tribunes like Churchill or Clemenceau be made to look today on those television programmes of the *Spitting Image* type which daily clutter the screens of the world's democracies with their gesticulating, inept political clones?

And after being put through the audiovisual mill in this way, would these statesmen still have enough charisma to mobilize populations and, ultimately, save democracy from pure and simple disappearance? *One may legitimately doubt it.* Once this question on the future of *political representation* has been raised, one can better understand that the dream of most of the major parties is to have members of parliament who are so 'soft', so much like silent soap stars, that no grotesque puppet could be made of them, no stupid comment attributed to them.

Here again, the Americans were the innovators, with a John Fitzgerald Kennedy – as rich, young, tanned and relaxed as the Great Gatsby – who won the presidential race in 1960 in front of 85 million TV viewers of both sexes, thanks to a live head-to-head debate with the physically rather unattractive Richard Nixon.

Ronald Reagan, an ageing Hollywood matinée idol, was still an imposing figure and his wife Nancy had a faultless figure. Jimmy Carter, fine fellow that he was, did a lot of jogging and, above all, looked disarmingly like the popular actor Mickey Rooney, one of the survivors from Hollywood's heyday.

George Bush was not unattractive and was very much the soap-opera figure. By contrast, his wife, with the robust physique of a dynamic grandmother, had to atone for this before the whole nation by mocking her own appearance.

Bill Clinton was first elected because he looked like Kennedy and because Hillary, his wife, was believed to have undergone various forms of plastic surgery. The popular media then set about their only daughter, a pleasant adolescent of thirteen but not exactly prepossessing. She had to modify her appearance to enable her father to win victory in the presidential election of 1996. These examples have been followed elsewhere and political supermodels have increased in number in recent years the world over.

And, indeed, Nixon was already of the opinion in the early 1970s that the presidents of the great powers were no longer really essential to the internal life of nations.

In other words, the president and the representatives of a nation would, once elected, cease to address themselves to that nation. They would, all in all, go with the general flow of the silent revolution of the audiovisual world.

So the team which trained Clinton for the last election got him to *speak as fast as possible*. Obeying strict television rules, he had to be able to **say everything** on a particular theme in less than ninety seconds – before going on to say nothing at all about it after he was elected.

But if you step out of line, you lose your place. New political mutants have recently appeared on our screens, such as Benjamin Netanyahu, Jörg Haider, Tony Blair. Apart from a visually correct physical appearance, these characters have understood that in a rapidly globalizing world there is no longer, *strictly speaking*, either Right or Left, and that, since the fall of the Berlin Wall, these things literally no longer have any meaning. All that remains is the great audiovisual dilemma, the conflict between the soft (the word) and the hard (the image).

Unlike the general run of the representatives of the old parties which are collapsing all around, these new political supermodels will speak a language which is 'hard' and impactful.

If the old leaders were concerned to please by correcting their appearance, jiving, jogging, etc., the new supermodels also know how to do this, but, in addition, in the great political and social silence of populations left to their own devices by their own leaders, *they speak*. And their speech is not addressed to any collective unconscious, but to that new state of consciousness which the instantaneous violence of universal communication at every second implies.

The talk of gathering together and drawing closer
together now gives way to a language which banishes,
excludes, rejects and divides . . . Such a backlash and such
repercussions are contained by definition within the technologies of acceleration. And terrorism and advertising
have long built their doctrine on such media violence.

From now on, it will be no use saying 'no'; they will
hear 'yes'.

Chapter 9

After the tragedy of the Apollo XIII capsule and the mid-air explosion of the Challenger shuttle, the Mir space station provides in its turn an illustration of the generalized accident that has befallen the adventure of space exploration.

Circumterrestrial space has at last become in everyone's eyes what it actually has been for the past thirty years: *a cosmic dustbin*, the dump where the astronautical industry's rubbish is deposited.

However, before it began to string together its long series of technical breakdowns over the course of 1997, this *Titanic* station had as early as 1991 instituted another type of accident with the Soviet *Ozon* mission: *the time accident*, the accident of that historic time of which Andrej Ujica's documentary *Out of the Present* depicts the succeeding episodes.

One of the cosmonauts, Sergei Krikalev, who ultimately remained in orbit against his will for ten long months, can be seen to have anticipated not only the *acceleration of his country's history* – with the collapse of the Soviet Union and the return of Holy Russia – but also *the acceleration of reality*. In fact the Mir space station is now merely a *monument among the stars*. As a cosmic ruin, it is, like the Pyramids, beginning to show its great age: eleven years. It is becoming loaded with memory and it is showing its obsolescence, not to mention the confusion on the part of those aboard, accused of all evils as they are by the orbital power of the City of the Stars.

By contrast with the great inter-sidereal dream of Wernher von Braun, the Russian space station reveals the fall from grace of a caste of stellar navigators elevated to heroic status for nearly half a century for the purposes of the military-industrial complex.

After the catastrophic collapse of the USSR, reality is reasserting itself. The era of political science fiction is coming to an end and the techno-scientific myth of the industrial omnipotence of man in space is imploding.

Hence the determined struggle to preserve Mir on the part of the last great world power, and also the PR launch on the Internet of the Mars Pathfinder operation, with its cute little robot.

Here again, time has passed. The 'cosmic illusion' has become derisory – a 'comic' illusion.

With the successive reverses met with by the passengers on this rusty 'vessel', which is due for the breaker's yard, Mir is another kind of Red Square Mausoleum. Following the example of the Chernobyl nuclear power plant, whose ruin led up to the end of the Soviet Union, the premature decaying of the Mir space station is the premonitory sign of an imminent collapse of the progressive myth of the conquest of the stars by humanity – of that cosmism which stepped into the void left by communism's decline at the end of the 1980s.

But today the last word is with the laws of astrophysics: *the sidereal void remains a void* and the current demythification of the glorious future of astronautics is probably more important for the history of our societies than the demythification of Marxism-Leninism.

After the fall of the Berlin Wall, we now see a whole swathe of techno-scientific positivism crumbling away noiselessly, with the ruination of the first **zenithal historic monument**.

Since the beginning of the 1990s, with the end of the Cold War and the geopolitics of the Eastern and Western blocs, we have been seeing not only the unfreezing, the decomposition of the old Soviet empire, but also the collapse of the *astronautical empire* – in spite of the endless proliferation of observation and telecommunications satellites.[1]

Being based on the advance research of men like Hermann Oberth, to which the ruins of Peenemünde still bear witness, the astronautics industry is today taking on a new complexion, orientating itself, as is the case throughout the field of production, towards the automation of space probes and other astronomical reconnaissance devices, so proving the inventor of tele-technologies V.K.

---

1 The New China Agency announced that, on Monday 1 September 1997, the Chinese rocket Long March 2.III put into orbit two Iridium satellites for the American Motorola Corporation. This network is to comprise in total sixty-six satellites of this type, twenty-four of which were already in orbit by late 1997.

Zworykin right when he declared in the 1930s that the future of electronic television consisted in its one day being made into the 'telescope of the future' by installing TV cameras on rockets, the alleged conquest of space thus never being anything more than a mere conquest of *the image of space* for a world of TV viewers. All this explains today the undeniable success of both the 'Martian chronicles' of the Sojourner robot and the disastrous saga of the Mir space station.

'I feel as though I'm on the fo'c'sle of Christopher Columbus's caravel, reaching the coasts of America,' marvelled a French astronomer on the Voyager 2 expedition, as the space probe reached the vicinity of Neptune.

Launched barely twenty years ago, the Voyager 1 and Voyager 2 probes have today travelled almost 6 billion miles at more than 40,000 miles per hour – *astronomical* figures which have, however, no meaning for us Earth creatures.

According to NASA, which is responsible for their launch, the performances of these *automatic spacecraft* might be said to represent one of the finest adventures of the space age: '*an achievement greater than sending a man into space or landing on the moon*'.

'These two 815 kg robots,' which have cost far less than the space shuttle, '*have taught us much more about the solar system than all the astronomers since Ptolemy put together*.'[2]

---

2 'Les Voyager fêtent leurs vingt ans aux frontières du système solaire'; *Le Monde*, 4 September 1997.

In space, it has definitely been the case for some time now that human beings are just an additional handicap.

The extra cost which astronauts represent makes them like contemporary proletarians in the great global companies. Sooner or later they will have to be dismissed, since, there also, hyper-productivity requires **automation** and a slimmed-down workforce.

If, for example, we believe Edward Stone, the director of the NASA centre responsible for carrying out automatic probes and the man at the origin of the Voyager programme,[3] these robots were supposed to observe only two planets, but the wealth of data garnered when Jupiter and Saturn were overflown in 1979 and 1981 made the Americans decide to extend their mission to the bounds of our galaxy, '*where no humanly produced instrument has ever gone to make measurements*'.[4]

The word is out. The point is not so much now to *explore* as to *measure*. And in this particular 'Star Wars', there is a future for the *tête chercheuse*.[5]

The disappointments of the cosmonauts of the Mir space station marvellously illustrate the discredit into which men at work have fallen – those voyagers on 'manned flights' who are not content merely to *read the gauges*, but wish to *gauge the full reality* of the world and what lies beyond it.

Surely this reflects once more the baneful influence of the technical rat race?

---

3 Edward C. Stone is the director of NASA's Jet Propulsion Laboratory (JPL) at Pasadena (Trans).

4 'Les Voyager . . .'.

5 The French term means both a pioneering researcher and a homing device. (Trans.)

'Acceleration weighs more heavily than work itself,' wrote Ernst Jünger. 'Growing haste is a symptom of a world turned into figures.'[6]

Today, beneath the very extremism of the results of research in the fields of physics and biophysics, doubt is creeping in, not only regarding the nature of progress, but as to what is becoming of 'science'.

Troubled by the development of 'accidents', some researchers are even becoming wary of their own work and are desperately trying to set some limits beyond which they will not go, thus bringing about the 'integral accident' of positivism.

'Behind the unquenchable thirst of scientific speculation lies more than mere curiosity. The first steps on the moon did, admittedly, advance knowledge, but they disappointed our hopes,' wrote Jünger once again. 'Space travel can lead to other goals than the ones it sets itself.'[7]

With the opposing sagas of the Mir space station and the Mars Pathfinder probe, this sudden disheartening effect of science is solidly back on the agenda.

In a recent interview Claude Allègre, the French minister for 'research and technology', declared: 'We were clearly on the wrong track with manned flight. On the other hand, I'm convinced that the exploration of Mars or Venus offers genuine scientific prospects.'

An official declaration in these terms amounts to a declaration of war on the already ancient company of

---

6 Ernst Jünger, *Siebzig verweht*, vol. 1, Klett-Cotta, Stuttgart, 1980, p. 402.
7 Ibid, p. 230.

astronauts – a challenge to which Jean-Loup Chrétien, the French space-flight veteran (aged fifty-nine), reacted by readying himself to join the Mir space station.

And a similar response can be seen from Senator John Glenn (aged seventy), the American pioneer of orbital flight, who requested readmission to the space programme to carry out a *shuttle mission* aimed at '*studying the effects of weightlessness on old age*'.

'*Exile is a long insomnia*,' wrote Victor Hugo, who well knew what he was talking about.

Is this, then, the end of extra-terrestrial emancipation, an end to the dream of humanity's great cosmic escape?

If this were actually the case, the present globalization of history would also be the closure, the end of scientific positivism.

Cosmonauts who, in the early years of the space race, had to play second fiddle to *laboratory animals* (Laika the dog, monkeys and various other 'guinea pigs'), are now, at the end of the twentieth century, in the same position with regard to *automatic machines*. They are faced with the domestic robots which are most probably set to take over from them.

In this context, it is easier to understand the hype there has been – in connection with the Internet – for that 'virtual space' which is destined tomorrow to supplant the 'real space' of the cosmos.

After the computer and the chess-player, the moment has perhaps come for us to give way to the 'bachelor machines' . . .

CHAPTER 10

'The aircraft brushes the ground and the ground opens it up more daintily than a gourmet peeling his fig. . . . With cinematic slow-motion, the most violent impact, the most lethal accident seems as gentle as a series of caresses.'[1] The film can also be run backwards. The fragments of the wreckage of the aircraft are then put back together again before our eyes with all the precision of the pieces of a jigsaw puzzle. The plane emerges unharmed from the dust cloud, which disappears, and, in conclusion, rises from the ground in reverse, before disappearing from the screen as though nothing had happened.

When it was claimed at the beginning of the twentieth century that *cinema represented a new age for humanity*, people did not realize how true this was.

In cinema, not only does nothing stop but, most important, nothing necessarily has any direction or sense, since

---

1 Paul Morand, *L'Homme pressé*, Gallimard, Paris, 1929.

on the screens *physical laws are reversed*. The end can become the beginning, the past can be transformed into the future, the right can be the left, the bottom the top, etc.

In a few decades, with the lightning progress made by industrial cinema, humanity has unwittingly passed into an era of directionlessness, of nonsense, into an age of what Americans call the 'shaggy dog story'. In slow-motion or speeded up, here or elsewhere, everywhere and nowhere, with cinematic optics and its very special effects, not only was humanity knocked out of kilter, but it began to see double.

Henceforth, what the acceleration of physical movement partially denied to the familiar gaze would be found on the screen within everyone's reach. The mechanics of bird flight or the galloping of horses, the ultra-rapid trajectories of projectiles, undetectable movements of air or water, the fall of bodies, the deflagration of matter, etc. And also, conversely, what was hidden in the extreme natural slowness of things: the germination of plants, the opening of flowers, biological metamorphoses, etc. – and you could see all these things in the order in which they happened or some other order, as you wished.

From the late nineteenth century onwards, the objectivity of the old scientific observation was to be shamefully compromised by this new imagery and the great concern of this 'cinedramatic age' (Karl Kraus) would become the conquest of this 'beyond' of the visible, this hidden face of our planet – no longer hidden by great distances, which were now mastered, but by Time itself – by its *extra-temporality* rather than its *extra-territoriality*.

This unprecedented fusion/confusion of the visible and

the invisible cannot but remind us of the origins of popular cinema as a music-hall or fairground attraction, which found its place, from 1895 onwards, between the stands of the illusionists and the stalls of genuine impecunious scientists, those 'mathemagicians' who performed their tricks of 'entertaining physical science' at fairgrounds.

In the words of Robert Houdin, a conjuror, but also a designer, in the nineteenth century, of androids and optical equipment, 'Illusionism is an art entirely concerned with taking advantage of the visual limits of the onlooker by attacking his innate capacity to distinguish between the real and what he believes to be real and true, thus inducing him *to believe firmly in that which does not exist.*'

Today, when an illusionist like David Copperfield (a disciple and admirer of Houdin) wants to perform his magic tricks in front of the cameras, he has the greatest difficulty not only making them credible, but above all making them *extraordinary* – not for want of skill, but because the field of public credulity has expanded considerably in recent years, keeping step, indeed, with the progress of the mass media. The move from a few hours of television a day to twenty-four-hour TV, but more especially the 'see-it-now' culture of real-time television, has reinforced in viewers – particularly the youngest among them – what are known as 'states of delusional conviction'.[2]

To astonish the audience, Copperfield will in future have to make not a dove disappear, but a Boeing – or something even bigger.

---

2 Absolute certainty inaccessible to any criticism and resistant even to the clearest of evidence.

Similarly, with regard to the surprising collective suicide of the Heaven's Gate sect, no one has really asked how these computer experts came to believe themselves capable of conjuring themselves away *physically* into an eternal realm, aided by a particular astronomic conjuncture.

But this does not seem so extravagant if we remember the slogan launched live on television on 21 July 1969 by Neil Armstrong, the first man to set foot on the surface of the moon: 'One small step for [a] man, one giant leap for mankind.'

On domestic television screens, the **real** small step looked like a vague little hop. Conversely, the **virtual** giant leap was more than 200,000 miles in length and 650 million people on Earth had the illusion of accomplishing it at the same moment. So 650 million people had entered weightlessness in their own homes, 'with a sense of having taken part in a great epic of exploration', as an American journalist was to write. Today, there would be billions *believing that.*

All because mechanics – all forms of mechanics (kinetic, wave, statistical, etc.) – have demonstrated mathematically that they were capable of freeing humanity from the physical constraints of the real world, and of its dimensions, which are supposed to be opposed to its potentialities and the worst of which is thought to be **time**.

It is not, then, a Boeing which our mathemagicians propose to make vanish, but the **living Earth**; and it is its **metaphysical double** which they are progressively unveiling to us. A dead star, rapidly dubbed cyberworld or cyberspace, whereas the name cybertime would better suit this nebula, this by-product of an illusionism which, since earliest antiquity, has prospered from *the public's* *visual limitations by destroying their capacity to distinguish between the real and what they believe to be real and true* . . . Like those Greek magicians who, according to Plato, claimed even in their day to be able to recreate the planet at will.

In this Lewis Carroll-style novel, **evil** might be said to have become the **real** through the multitude of its analogue systems. **Good** would consist in eradicating these, in pushing them to shameful excess.

We are even seeing, under the pressure of advertising, the formation of a new bellicose mood, a kind of **coalition of opposites**. Everyone now believes they have to take a single, extra-terrestrial line in which, against all logic, the materialist espouses the theologian, the scientist unites with the journalist, the biologist mates with the fascist, the capitalist with the socialist, the colonialist with the decolonized, etc. From the pan-destruction of the world announced more than a century ago by Bakunin to the crazed hurrahs of the European Futurists, 'breaking their contacts with the contemptible Earth', who were soon to hand on the baton to the Hiroshima atomic scientists, with the recent psychokinetic madness of Internauts still to come . . . *the war of the worlds* was declared long ago, whether we like it or not, and, more than in any other war, *its first casualty* is truth.

Just as the fierce Homeric lyrics, with their fantastical population of bloodthirsty gods, superhuman heroes and morphing monsters, prefigured the great land, sea and air invasions of antiquity and our own times, why, since science has become a romance, should we not take seriously modern science-fiction tales which are obsessed with the imminent arrival of a new race of ruthless conquerors, of murderers on a grand scale – the conquerors of *the Time war*, that ultimate mythic odyssey in which the invaders' will to overlordship would be exerted not upon geographical distances, but in perturbations of a spatio-termporal vortex?

Let us again remember Hiroshima, more a *crime against matter* than a *war crime*, which was received in the United States as a 'gift from God', and more recently such ultra-rapid conflicts as the Falklands/Malvinas in 1982 or the Gulf in 1991. These, it was said, were 'war games', image wars, but, more than this, they were metaphysical conflicts between the real and the virtual.

However, let us come back to popular cinema, which from the end of the nineteenth century onwards invited us to revisit the planet thanks to 'world news'. We were to visit it now not for its tourist charms, its natural marvels, but as a huge terrain for all manner of calamities and catastrophes – fires, shipwrecks, hurricanes, earthquakes, wars and genocides . . .

The accident, which is by its nature rare, was henceforth to be part of daily life. And, even better, as in the case of Paul Morand's aircraft, it could be transformed into an object of visual delectation, which could be served up again at will and which, as it turned out, the general public could not get enough of.

The pan-destruction of the world would no longer be an elite entertainment reserved, Nero-style, for a few potentates. With the cinema, it would become a mass spectacle and, one might say, *the true popular art of the twentieth century*. A century in which, as the Surrealists asserted, 'all that was previously called **art** seemed to have become paralytic'. And indeed, *without movement, what would accidents be?*

Just before the carnage of 1914, American cinema of the Mack Sennett type offered it up for our consumption as comedy, with those short slapstick films in which hosts of vehicles of different kinds (trains, cars, planes and ships) collided, crashed, smashed, exploded and were quickly repaired in a collection of catastrophes from which the heroes emerged without pain and strangely unharmed.

'A joyful tragedy intended for a recent and as yet uncreated humanity,' prophesied Luis Buñuel.

The real accident would soon have the simulated one for company. 'Disaster movies' aimed at a mass audience would take as their model the wreck of the *Titanic* or the San Francisco earthquake – and this is not to mention the surfeit of war films.

'Jumping, falling and sweating!' This is how the actor Harrison Ford recently summed up his job. The achievement of star status itself would seem to be based not on talent or good looks any more, but on the risks taken for the camera by a whole host of stuntmen brought in from the fairgrounds and circuses: trick riding, controlled falls, suspended accidents and suicidal exploits, leading, with the coming of 'live' transmission, to the 'confessional' TV programme, to the so-called *reality show*, which shades over, at the edges, into the *snuff movie*.

What would James Dean have been, for the public at large, without his Porsche – or Ayrton Senna without his Ferrari, or Princess Diana without the fatal Mercedes at the end of her tragic road movie?

Shortly after the wild funeral accorded to the Brazilian motor-racing champion came that of the Princess of Wales, which resembled nothing so much as a huge political plebiscite, with the Union Jack flying over Buckingham Palace and the Queen of England forced to make due apology before the cameras and declare *her people united in an example to the world.*

But what world and what people? And can we still speak in these terms of the billions of TV viewers who long ago got out of their depth and have since drowned in the mass media?

Her poor Majesty, who is still at the horse-racing stage, and her son Charles with his watercolours and organic vegetable growing, like a latter-day Marie-Antoinette tending her sheep in the Petit Trianon.

Poor Labour Party, which, after sounding the alarm, is now afraid it might hear the death-knell of the British monarchy and soon also its own – the death-knell of the old political class. Has not one of Tony Blair's political advisers, Geoff Mulgan, just published a book entitled *Life after Politics,* in which he claims, as many others have done, that with the Internet and globalization, 'Modern citizens simply take it for granted that they have a right to run their own lives, to have a say on how decisions are made, and to create their own meanings'?[3]

Poor President Clinton, who was solemnly warned of this in June 1997 by the self-proclaimed 'masters of the digital universe', the members of the Business Software Alliance, who came to present an ultimatum to the White House.

This is the first of the markers put down, they say, for

3 Geoff Mulgan, *Life after Politics,* Fontana (HarperCollins), London, 1997, p. x.

that 'democratic capitalism' which, with its universal network, should very soon escape the existing institutions and in short order bring about the disappearance of all intermediate bodies, be they economic, political, judicial or cultural.

More 'down to earth', no doubt, and, more significantly, a product of the older 'eco' generation, Ted Turner, the boss of CNN and vice-president of Time Warner, declared himself a 'defender of the planet' and called on President Clinton to pay the USA's debt to the United Nations, while at the same time announcing that he was giving a billion dollars to the organization for 'its charitable work'. A take-over bid of a new, extra-terrestrial kind?

At the end of this summer of 1997 of our 'shaggy dog story', we shall further note the ceremony which took place in September at Star City near Moscow when the two unfortunate members of the former crew of the Mir space station, after being threatened with the direst penalties, each received in the end *a plot of land* as a reward – a little bit of this living planet which had very nearly become, for them, *a lost world*. As it is for those Brazilian peasants of the MST (the Social Movement of Agricultural Workers) who are dying in their hundreds at the moment 'for a patch of land, a crust of bread, and so that their children do not become outlaws'.

CHAPTER 11

A few years ago a troupe of Italian mime artistes offered Parisian spectators the curious spectacle of a dozen grown men wearing nappies and bibs and bustling around on stage, stumbling, fighting, falling, screaming, cuddling, playing ring o' roses, shutting each other out of the circle and so on . . . These burlesque figures were like neither children nor adults. They were false adults or false children – or perhaps caricatures of children. It was not easy to say precisely which.

Similarly, when Bill Gates, who is in his forties but has the outward appearance of an adolescent, ventures to declare publicly, 'It may be, you never know, that the universe exists only for me! If it were true, I have to admit I would enjoy that!', then you wonder whether the boss of Microsoft does not also suffer from a kind of *dimensional derangement*, and whether this universe of which he speaks is not, like that of the nursery, the scaled-down world of the toys and games of an overgrown spoilt child.[1]

---

1 *VSD*, Christmas and New Year special edition, 1997.

As early as the first half of the twentieth century, Witold Gombrowicz and a number of his contemporaries had noted that the mark of modernity was not growth or human progress, but rather the refusal to grow up. 'Immaturity and infantilism are the most effective categories for defining modern man,' Gombrowicz wrote. After the telescopic metamorphoses of Alice, we had reached the Peter Pan stage – the stage of the child stubbornly determined to escape his future.

It seemed no longer possible to make the transition to adulthood, which was primordial in ancient societies, in a civilization in which everyone carried on playing without any age limit.

In a few years, social or political responsibilities, military duties, the world of work, etc. would be swept away and soon anyone or any activity which did not have aspects of puerility would be dubbed 'elitist' and rejected as such.

The general tendencies of the market and of mass production were to be gravely affected by this and we were to pass inexplicably from the industrial to the post-industrial age, from the *real* to the *virtual*, thus fulfilling the hopes of a resolutely immature society.

To prefer the illusions of networks – drawing on the absolute speed of electronic impulses, which give, or claim *to give, instantaneously what time accords only gradually* – means not only making light of geographical dimensions, as the acceleration of rapid vehicles has been doing for more than a century now, but, above all, hiding the future in the ultra-short time-span of telematic 'live transmission'. It means *making the future no longer appear to exist by having it happen now.*

No future – the eternal childhood of the Japanese

'*otakus*' of the eighties – refusing to *wake up to a life* by leaving the world of the digital imagination, by exiting from *manga* land.

In a book of reminiscences completed on 22 February 1942, shortly before his suicide at Petropolis (Brazil), Stefan Zweig described pre-1914 Europe and in particular the Viennese society in which he had grown up. He related how the obsessive concern with security had come to amount virtually to a social system in which, in spite of heightened nationalist tensions, the stability of political and economic institutions, insurance of all kinds, the durability of families and the severe control of manners were supposed to protect everyone from the blows of fate. Zweig wrote:

> It is reasonable that we, who have long since struck the word 'security' from our vocabulary as a myth, should smile at the optimistic delusion of that idealistically blinded generation, that the technical progress of mankind must connote an unqualified and equally rapid moral ascent.

A little further on, he added, 'We who, each new day, expect things worse than the day before.'[2]

What concerns us here is the treatment reserved for youth in this kind of progressive and, simultaneously, 'safety-first' society.

---

2 Stefan Zweig, *The World of Yesterday*, trans. Cedar and Eden Paul, Cassell, London, 1987, p. 15.

The child and the adolescent were in fact regarded as part of the potential danger which the future harboured. They were therefore treated harshly. Their upbringing and schooling were quasi-military in character (Zweig said his school had 'a barracks-like quality');[3] they had arranged marriages, dowries and inherited positions. In this way youth was kept away from business matters, in a state of perpetual dependency, with legal majority being set at the age of twenty-three and a man in his forties still being regarded as suspect. In order to be granted a responsible position, he would have to 'disguise' himself as a solid, staid citizen, if not indeed as an old man, with a long beard and a reassuring 'corporation'.

As a consequence, Zweig, who was to be a frequent visitor of Freud's, believed more or less that the famous doctor owed his theories in large part to the excesses of the Austrian social system, such as, for example, the very Viennese idea of a childhood that was without 'innocence' and potentially dangerous for the adult (were not perverse individuals referred to as 'overgrown children', afflicted with 'psychical infantilization'?). And even more so to his attention to the desire shared by an impatient youth to 'break the (cultural, linguistic and moral) protective shackles' of a safety-minded society, seen as representing a typically paternal type of oppression, the abolition of taboos being in reality the abolition of the exorbitant privileges of omnipotent old men, fearful of the future from excess of caution.

*

---

3 Ibid., p. 34.

This makes it easier to understand the violent reactions of Karl Kraus, who called psychoanalysts the '*dregs of humanity*', or of Kafka speaking of psychoanalysis as '*an unmitigated error*'.

The fact is that beside – right alongside – the delusion of the *class struggle* (which itself ended up sinking into the neo-conservatism of gangsterish nomenclaturas governed by old men), another revolution was taking place less openly, a revolution which came out of the privately conducted *generational struggle* and a physiological war as immemorial as that between the sexes or ethnic groups.

The as yet sparse avant-garde of that youthful revolution was first to storm *cultural power* – and to do so, let us note, essentially in the name of *actes manqués* (from Romanticism to Dada or Surrealism). However, this emancipation of a youth which will later be dubbed illiterate would be accelerated by the very excesses of this devastating century. As Jules Romains wrote, 'without the extreme youth of the combatants in the First World War, slaughters such as occurred at Verdun (almost 700,000 dead) would not have been possible'. And he added, 'young people do not think of the future. They are not easily moved to pity. They know how to be ferocious and laugh all the while.'

We may turn the argument around and look for an explanation in the old men who had dragged them there, from Franz-Joseph I, the emperor of Austria, who unleashed the murderous conflict at the age of eighty-four, to Georges Clemenceau, the promoter of decimation *pour l'exemple*, who was getting on for eighty. And we should not forget also the rationalism of a new military bureaucracy which was capable of managing the whole of the male population as an exercise in health administration, on the basis of an age criterion in which the youngest were automatically sacrificed.[4]

Later, *when even worse infamies than those which had preceded were constantly occurring*, Hannah Arendt would lucidly observe this wave of nihilism, which one might be tempted to date historically to Hitler, but also to Marx or Nietzsche; this revolution of old values which are immediately declared as new values – thus creating a *reverse historical process*.

Nietzsche was not a philosopher, nor Hitler a statesman. Both were, rather, the paranoid interpreters of the apocalyptic ultimatum of youth battling with the *irreversibility of time*: 'For the Earth and what is in it there shall be no more delay!'[5]

'No future' – the great hecatombs of industrial wars and revolutions finally answered the prayers of an entire younger generation, since they had the twofold merit of destroying its (moral, cultural and social) past, and sparing

---

4 Paul Virilio, *Speed and Politics: An Essay on Dromology*, trans. Mark Polizzotti, Semiotext(e), New York, 1986.

5 I have followed the author's own translation of this verse from Revelation here, which is slightly at variance with the standard English translations and with the French translation by Louis Segond. The text from the Revised Standard Version is as follows: 'And the angel whom I saw standing on sea and land lifted up his right hand to heaven and swore by him who lives for ever and ever, who created heaven and what is in it, the Earth and what is in it, and the sea and what is in it, that there should be no more delay. . . .' (Revelation 10:5–6, *The RSV Interlinear Greek-English New Testament*, Samuel Bagster and Sons, London, 1972, p. 985). (Trans.)

it the *shadow* cast by a future seen as the irremediable coming of a hated old age.

When peace was momentarily restored, the escapees from the massacres carried on pursuing their race against the clock, their attack on time.

After the *artistes maudits* of the nineteenth century came the lost generations of the so-called roaring twenties. With them we were to see a democratization of the trend. We went from Scott Fitzgerald to Kerouac and a Beat generation with suicidal and criminal tendencies; then came the angelism of Woodstock and the final upsurge of 1968 where, as Hannah Arendt foresaw, *imagination would not come to power*.[6]

After them would come the enforced idleness of the new losers and the various other junkies, the swelling ranks of the social dregs of a post-industrial world.

The dreams of liberation of a formerly oppressed youth, avid for change, have in fact always led to dictatorships and repressive paramilitary systems. After Hitler and Stalin in the Soviet Union – even though after the First World War that country was seen as the Mecca of this youthful cultural revolution – we come to the new technological nannying offered to the world by an American nation which has plunged into a complete globalitarian frenzy. And we do so merely because the adverts for its old traditional products (Coke, jeans, Hollywood, Mickey Mouse, etc.) paradoxically present the image of a *young country*. Young or, more accurately, *infantile*.

---

6 Lecture delivered on 30 October 1970 at the New School for Social Research.

In fact, the citizens of that great nation are undergoing a process Edgar Allan Poe had foreseen in the early nineteenth century (which will soon afflict all the world's citizens): 'Even while he [Man] stalked a God in his own fancy, an infantine imbecility came over him. . . . Arts – the Arts – arose supreme, and, once enthroned, cast chains upon the intellect which had elevated them to power.'[7]

If, as Zweig asserted, the older generations, not without naivety, confused techno-scientific and moral progress, for the new generations, who were eager to abrogate all culture and all morality (as a theory of the ends of human actions), *technologies would inevitably advance alone*, leaving behind them a humanity without a future, assuming definitively pre-pubescent airs – the critical age in business still being the forties, though now not for admitting candidates to responsible positions, but for ejecting them because they are too old.

This may also be taken to explain the development of *automatism* as the ultimate substitute offered by technological progress for the parapraxes of a resolutely immature social body.

When one recalls, for example, ancient democracies and the draconian control exerted directly by the citizens over the leaders they elected, it is remarkable to note that

---

7 Edgar Allan Poe, 'The Colloquy of Monos and Una', in *Collected Works: Tales and Sketches 1831–1842*, edited by Thomas Ollive Mabbott with the assistance of Eleanor D. Kewer and Maureen C. Mabbott, The Belknap Press of Harvard University Press, Cambridge (Mass.) and London, 1978. (Trans.)

today, at the pinnacle of the state, *irresponsibility* has become a right, a privilege shielding the governing classes from parliamentary or judicial control with regard to the acts accomplished in the course of their duties (except where otherwise specified in the constitution).

As we know, this staggering situation of an *irresponsible head of state* was reinforced by the Cold War when the automatic nature of responses to nuclear strikes had greatly downgraded the interventions of human decision-makers.

In the early months of 1998 this condition of irresponsibility was to take a grotesque turn when the president of the world's most powerful state was in danger of being turned out of his job for a tiny lie about his sex life and yet, at the same time, was allowed, with impunity, to order an Arab state to be reduced to rubble (this he could not really be held responsible for; that is to say, he could not be seen as truly conscious of it and guilty) in a ludic society which had been not at all reluctant, some forty years ago, to schedule the nuclear death of the planet as though it were a board game.

To confound the multi-media and the political opponents who had put him in the hot seat, it would be sufficient for President Clinton, in a keenly awaited State of the Union address, to speak in sustained praise of the superiority of American military technologies, thus forcing his opponents to applaud him on pain of having their conservative voters desert them.

Shortly afterwards, he went even further down the path of presidential *irresponsibility* by proposing to automate reprisal strikes against the enemies of American interests in the world.

To complete this curious picture of general illogicality, and at a time when it was believed that a dangerous conflict was looming, the government of the United States announced on 10 February 1998 that it had decided not to unleash its attack on Iraq before the end of the winter Olympics, which were taking place at the same time in Japan. That way, TV viewers would not be discommoded by a mix of contradictory images, improperly mingling the euphoria of the winter games with the far from reassuring sights of a new Gulf War, which would have forced them to zap endlessly between channels, adversely affecting the interests of the sponsors of these various lucrative activities. The intelligent intervention of Kofi Annan, a skilful African diplomat, was happily to resolve this situation of highly technological imbecility.

'They are a white family, four dummies displayed entirely naked, standing hand in hand like a decorative lace pattern. All four of the figures – the father, mother, son and daughter – have been designed to have exactly the same height: 4 feet 8 inches,' wrote Élisabeth Lebovici on 25 April 1993 in *Libération*. And she added:

> This vaguely Hollywoodian scenario – *Honey, I enlarged the kids* (which makes them look completely stupid) and *I shrank the parents* (they are literally small-scale dummies) – concocted by Californian artist Charles Ray, inevitably prompts a rather cheeky question: are not average Americans perhaps overgrown children? But the message offered by the Whitney Museum of American Art in New York in the context of its 1993 Biennale is

probably harder to swallow: is there an American
art? It is a question of rethinking the canons in
force in the American cultural world.[8]

After the ideological collapse of the Soviet bloc in the
1990s, it is time to remember that, for the United States, all
culture is *historically* part of an anthropology of a colonialist kind, rather than being part of artistic activities which
might be specific to that country.

Charles Ray's installation with its four human figures
gives us an idea, then, of the future of world culture as
conceived by the Americans. After the more or less suc-
cessful assimilation of the sexes, the races and the colours,
the generations will be assimilated. They will be 'hybridized'
through a levelling down, a little bit like those pygmy tribes
who cut off their taller enemies' legs to bring them down
to their level.

Let us imagine, for example, an adult and a small child
climbing a staircase. The child will not be able to cope
with the height of the steps and will rapidly be outdis-
tanced and left behind by the adult. By contrast, when
the adult and the child get into a lift together, they will
ascend at the same speed. Each in his way will be *dis-pro-
portioned.* The adult will have lost a little of his status of
'grown man' (we might even say he has grown younger
or smaller), whereas the child will have grown preco-
ciously or – why should we not see it this way? – will
have aged.

---

8 Charles Ray's mixed media installation is called *Family
Romance*. (Trans.)

With the proliferation of these kinds of technological servants (domestic objects, work tools, instruments of communication, armaments, vehicles, etc.), the adult man of the industrial age and, even more, of the post-industrial age, has progressively ceased not just to be a *centre of energy*, as Paul Valéry pointed out, but, by no longer putting his body into things (two per cent of the energy expended on Earth is bodily energy), he has ceased, most importantly, to measure the world by his own scale (in feet, inches, 'paces', power). In all senses of the term, man is no longer the *yardstick of the world*, or, as we used to say, he is no longer the *measure of all things*.

Let us be in no doubt about it, then, technological progress is merely completing the juvenile revolution of the past century. As with our Italian mime-artists, transformed into caricatures of children, play is now everywhere. After the civilization of the image, which was merely the civilization of the young illiterate's picture-book adapted for adult consumption, from industrial photography to the 'curvaceous' lines of pornographic comics, and on to the educational system and vocational training. To the gimmickification of the system of consumer goods, in which everyone finds themselves equipped with objects not so much built for use as subject to the changeable standards of immaturity. We feed on unhealthy, sugary foods to the point of indigestion and obesity. Gambling on the stock market – and the stakes involved – exceeds all actual material constraints. Anti-prohibition activists refer to drug-taking as a 'recreational activity' . . .

If marriage has become a precarious institution today, this is because newly-weds reject the abominable idea of *growing old together*, or, alternatively, because the immediacy of the present world prevents them from believing in any kind of lasting future.

In what is not so much the reconstructed as the de-constructed family, adults have childish whims and share the toys and other electronic equipment for which the young are so gifted. With their uncertain progeny they assume the position of partner, to the point indeed of paedophilia, since, as everyone knows, sex is *a wonderful toy*.[9]

Further accentuating this drift, the age of majority has been lowered over a few years from twenty-one to eighteen and now some members of parliament are suggesting it should be brought down to sixteen or even fifteen.

In this generalized loss of markers of age, children are, at a younger and younger age, abandoning daytime play, in the form of sport and recreation, for night-time street activities, moving out to join an immature world whose toys they demand, and to become the main actors in a revolution which was made for them. They will in their turn be ferocious and laugh all the while, stealing cars and motor-cycles, indulging in vandalism (toys are made to be broken), using weapons unthinkingly.

As they are beyond the reach of the law – i.e. legally irresponsible – and abandoned by divided, infantilized families, there will soon be millions of them (exploited in their work) in the various branches of criminal activity. Not forgetting the child-soldiers enrolled from the age of ten or twelve in resistance movements and pseudo-wars of liberation.

---

9 '*Un joujou extra*'. The reference is to a Jacques Dutronc pop song. (Trans.)

In February 1998 the United Nations counted thirty-eight wars or conflicts in the world, and estimated the number of such 'lost children' at 250,000. On the UN's initiative, some forty countries have tried in vain to raise to eighteen the minimum age for recruiting minors for combat, which was set in the 1990 convention at fifteen.

A convention on the rights of the child which was not, of course, signed by the United States, since it ran counter to that country's great project of hybridizing the generations.[10]

---

10 On the military proletarianization of children, both abandoned children and the offspring of slaves, see Virilio, *Speed and Politics*, p. 84.

CHAPTER 12

Every political revolution is a drama, but the coming technical revolution is without doubt more than just a drama. It is a *tragedy of knowledge*, the Babelish confusion of individual and collective bodies of learning.

As Aesop said of language, the Internet is both the best and the worst of things. It is the advance of a limitless – or almost limitless – communication; and at some point it is also the disaster – the meeting with the iceberg – for this *Titanic* of virtual navigation.

The cybernetics of the network of networks, the product of a 'techno-sophic' illusion contemporaneous with the end of the Cold War as 'end of history', is a techno-system of strategic communication which brings with it the *systemic risk* of a chain reaction of damage that will occur as soon as globalization has become effective.

There is no point today speculating on the regional character – or otherwise – of the recent Asian stock market crash. If the cybernetics of the financial market had actually been globalized, the crash of autumn 1997 would have been instantaneously planetary and the economic catastrophe would have been total.

Thus, after the *atom* bomb and the deployment for over forty years of generalized nuclear deterrence, the *information bomb* which has just exploded will very soon require the establishment of a new type of *deterrence* – in this case, a *societal* one, with 'automatic circuit-breakers' put in place capable of avoiding the over-heating, if not indeed the fission, of the social cores of nations.

With the real-time globalization of telecommunications – the unofficial model for which is provided by the Internet – the information revolution shows itself to be also a *systematic snooping operation*, which triggers a panic phenomenon of rumour and suspicion, and which is set to ruin the foundations of 'truth' in a professional ethics and hence the freedom of the press. Everyone can see this from the role of the Internet, for example, in the Clinton–Lewinsky scandal, with the doubts cast on the veracity of the facts asserted/denied, the uncontrollable development of a manipulation of sources and hence of public opinion itself – all of which are so many warning signs that prove the revolution of *real information* is also a revolution in *virtual disinformation* and hence in history as currently being written.

Radioactivity of the elements of matter, interactivity of the constituents of information – the harm done by irradiation is discreet and multifarious, at times amounting to general contamination.

The actors and tele-actors of the cybernetic telecommunications revolution, acting and interacting in real time, set a technical pace or tempo which now lords it over the properly historical importance of the *local time* of societies and countries. This works to the exclusive advantage of a *world time* which no longer belongs so much to the history of nations as to the abstraction of a **universal chrono-politics** for which no political representative is truly responsible, except for certain military general staffs in the case of *cyberwar being declared.*

What are we to say, for example, of researchers' silence on the role of the National Security Agency in the history of the development of the Internet? How are we to analyse today the resolve of the American State Department to make military strikes against a country which offends against the new world order – as it happens, Iraq – *automatic?*

Behind the libertarian propaganda for a *direct (live) democracy,* capable of renovating party-based *representative democracy,* the ideology of an *automatic democracy* is being put in place, in which the absence of deliberation would be compensated by a 'social automatism' similar to that found in opinion polls or the measurement of TV audience ratings.

A reflex democracy, without collective reflexion, in which conditioning would have greater importance than 'electoral campaigning' and in which the 'demonstrative' character of the party programmes would give way to the strictly 'monstrative' and spectacular character of a drilling of individual behaviour, the parameters of which were long ago tested out by advertising.

Moreover, has not the network of networks, established on the basis of the Arpanet system, which was designed to resist the electromagnetic effects of an atomic war, presented an occasion – since the Gulf War – for launching the very first *universal advertising campaign* for a systemic product which interests *no one in particular* and *everyone in general*?

The promotion of the Web and its on-line services, an unprecedented phenomenon of ideological contamination, no longer bears any resemblance to the marketing of a practical technology, such as the sale of a vehicle or even of some kind of broadcasting equipment (radio, television), since what is involved in this case is the *most immense enterprise of opinion transformation* ever attempted in 'peacetime', an undertaking which has scant regard for the collective intelligence or the culture of nations.

Hence, among other things, the general excessiveness – of the provisions of the Multilateral Agreement on Investment (MAI), for example, or of the NTM, the 'transatlantic free-trade project'.

These are globalitarian campaigns and they have about them the intensity of American propaganda for 'info-war', that *revolution in military affairs* initiated by the Pentagon at the end of the Cold War.

Yet one would understand nothing of the Internet and the future information superhighways if one forgot the interactive dimension of the arrangement and the birth of a real **comparative advertising** which is no longer content merely to vaunt the excellence of a particular product, but is concerned, first and foremost, to *impugn the commercial competitor*, to disarm the resistance of consumers, by denigrating their position, or merely their reticence.

Not content to satisfy the legitimate curiosity of the purchasers of their goods, the advertising agencies are now intent on calling for the *symbolic murder* of their competitors. Hence the decision of the European Parliament to adopt effective legislation against these 'campaigns of systematic denigration'.[1]

We should also point out that the Web can no longer be separated from the technical development which aims to replace the totality of *analogue* information by a digitalization of the knowledge media over the next ten years.

With the *digital* on the verge of winning out in all spheres of audiovisual production, the European Community is currently examining *a Green Paper on convergence.*

According to the authors of this report, the fact that a single technology – the digital – is used for different purposes (telephone, television or computers) should lead to a re-examination of the special treatment accorded to the Community's audiovisual sector and to that sector being brought solely under market control, as is the case with telecommunications.

The second strand in this *tentacular* convergence clearly concerns the Internet, with the idea that, on this network of American origin, since anything goes, future jurisdiction over the system should be solely a matter for the United States.

We are thus moving imperceptibly towards a sort of **image crash**.

---

1   In May 1998 Fashion-TV, a women's fashion chain founded by Adam Lisowski, took the Walt Disney Company (Europe SA) to court for spreading defamatory rumours, and for a 'campaign to blacken its name among the clients and partners of Fashion-TV', which might be explained by the imminent launch of a rival fashion chain by Disney. See *Le Nouvel Observateur*, 30 May 1998, TV supplement.

An eye for an eye – the competition between icons is currently on the agenda and that competition, in assuming worldwide proportions, is, like everything else in the era of the great planetary market-place, destabilizing for the regime of temporality of the whole of iconic information.

Screen against screen – the home computer *terminal* and the television *monitor* are squaring up to each other in a fight to dominate *the global perception market*, control of which will, in the near future, open up a new era both in aesthetics and in ethics.

'With 500,000 screens throughout the world tracking a totally computerized stock market, the Asian crash was watched everywhere as it happened,' declared a French trader in autumn 1997.

But when there are 5 million *live-cams* spread all over the world and several hundred million Internet users capable of observing them simultaneously at their consoles, we shall see the first **visual crash**, and so-called *television* will then give way to the generalized tele-surveillance of a world in which the famous *virtual bubble* of the financial markets will be supplanted by the *visual bubble* of the collective imaginary, with the attendant risk of the explosion of the information bomb announced back in the 1950s by Albert Einstein himself.

If, today, the *irrational* is amplified in the various sectors of financial globalization, it will flourish even more tomorrow in the field of the *globalization of the collective imaginary*, since the multiplier effect of the old television (responsible, among other things, for the Rodney King affair, the O.J. Simpson trial and the *post mortem* coronation of Princess Diana) will be infinitely reinforced by the **over-reactive** character of world tele-surveillance.

'The generalization of individual positions, when they are all moving in the same direction, generates unstable global conjunctures,' observed a CNRS analyst writing of the Asian crash. '*The rationality of individual behaviours makes for an overall irrationality.*'[2]

As **world** time ('live') takes over from the ancient, immemorial supremacy of the **local** time of regions, both the next step in *interactive* advertising and the even more fearsome conditions for *comparative* advertising between brands and investors are set to appear. This is a veritable cold civil war, a guerrilla war involving the symbolic execution of competitors, for which the European Council is set to give the go-ahead.

In this globalitarian conjuncture, the 'advertising space' is no longer to be found in the breaks between films or the TV slots between programmes: *it is now the real space-time of all communication.* Virtual inflation no longer relates solely to the economy of manufactured products, the financial bubble, but to the very understanding of our relation to the world.

As a result, the great '*danger to the system*' is no longer that of the bankruptcy of companies or banks in a chain reaction, such as we have recently seen in Asia, but the for-midable threat of a blinding, of a collective blindness on the part of humanity – the unprecedented possibility of a *defeat of facts* and hence a disorientation of our relation to reality.

The bankruptcy of phenomena, the catastrophic slump of the visible, from which economic and political *disinfor-mation* alone could derive advantage: with the *analogue*

---

2 André Orlan, *Le Monde*, 5 November 1997.

yielding its prerogatives to the *digital*, and with the recently achieved 'data compression' making it possible henceforth to speed up – that is to say, to concertina – our relation to reality . . . but to do so on condition that we accept the increasing impoverishment of sensory appearances.

In this way, with the progressive **digitalization** of audiovisual, tactile and olfactory information going hand in glove with the decline of immediate sensations, the *analogue resemblance* between what is close at hand and comparable would yield primacy to the *numerical probability* alone of things distant – of all things distant. And would in this way pollute our sensory ecology once and for all.

CHAPTER 13

Half a century ago, in 1948, Daniel Halévy published his
Essai sur l'accélération de l'histoire, in which he marked out
the great historical perspectives which lay before humanity
after Hiroshima:

> Poor old Earth, which we were happy in the
> eighteenth century to measure, and whose features,
> fauna and flora we were content to trace; poor old
> Earth, source of an even more intense contentment
> when we had succeeded in the nineteenth century
> in girding it with waves, making it a living, vibrant
> thing like a being, a soul!
>   Poor old humanity, obsessed with despotic
> visions, equipped with weapons which seem forged
> to make those very visions a reality!

Daniel Halévy, more perceptive in this than Francis
Fukuyama, already dimly saw that, far from bringing history to an end, techno-scientific progress was going to

blast away all delay, all duration, and that historical science would soon open up to a new **tempo**, a pace which should, at some stage not too far distant, speed up even the 'truth' of history:

> Just as, a quarter of a century ago, when Einstein put forward his relativist equations, human beings gave up understanding the overall *physical context* in which they live, we can see them today giving up understanding the overall *political context* in which their lives unfold.

What are we to say, at the end of the twentieth century, in the age of **globalization**, of this *refusal of understanding*, other than that it is going on before our very eyes, with the decline of the nation-state and the discrete revival in new forms of politics by the media, by the multi-media constituted by these networks and screens which show us the *acceleration of time*; the multi-media of that 'real time' of interchanges which performs the relativistic feat of compressing the 'real space' of the globe through the temporal compression of information and images of the world? Henceforth, *here no longer exists; everything is now*. The end of our history has not happened, but we do have the programmed end of the '*hic et nunc*' and the '*in situ*'.

The globalization of trade is not, then, *economic*, as has been the constant refrain since the development of the single market; it is, primarily, *ecological* and relates not merely to the pollution of **substances**, with, for example, the greenhouse effect in the atmosphere, but also to the pollution of **distances** and delays which make up the world of concrete experience.

In other words, globalization relates to the *dromospheric greenhouse effect* of confinement within the limit-acceleration of telecommunications.

'The time of the finite world is beginning,' declared Paul Valéry as early as the 1920s. With the 1980s, the world of finite time began. In the face of this sudden ending of all localized *durée*, the acceleration of history is running up against the barrier of real time, that universal *world time* which tomorrow will supplant all the local times which were capable *of making history*.

After the discovery, in the eighteenth century, of the *deep time* of those millions of years required for the geological concretion of the planet which bears us, we have today the invention of this *surface time* of the dromological reality-effect of remote action.

The *matter-time* of the hard geophysical reality of places gives way to this *light-time* of a virtual reality which modifies the very truth of all *durée*, thereby provoking, with the time accident, the acceleration of all reality: of things, living beings, socio-cultural phenomena.

What are we to say, for example, of the 'virtual communities' organized in networks around the Internet? There are already 70 million Internet users throughout the world, *communities of believers* 'tele-present' one to another thanks to the instantaneity – and, before long, the electronic ubiquity – of on-line cameras.

What, then, remains of the historical importance of the public space of the city in the era of this META-CITY in which the public image is king? An interactive image in commerce, education and the post-industrial enterprise, available at all times – and from one end to the other of our small planet.

Ultimately, it is not so much geography which is conditioned by globalization, but present and future history. *The acceleration of real time*, the limit-acceleration of the speed of light, not only dispels geophysical extension, the 'life-size' character of the terrestrial globe, but, first and foremost, it dispels the importance of the *longues durées* of the local time of regions, countries and the old, deeply territorialized nations.

By supplanting the 'chronological' successivity of local times, thanks to the instantaneity of a universal world time, tele-technologies over-expose not only all *activity*, by making it *interactive*, but also all *truth* and historical reality.

Past, **present** and **future** – that old tripartite division of the time continuum – then cedes primacy to the immediacy of a tele-presence which is akin to a new type of **relief**. This is a relief not of the material thing, but of the event, in which the fourth dimension (that of time) suddenly substitutes for the third: the material volume loses its geometrical value as an 'effective presence' and yields to an audiovisual volume whose self-evident 'tele-presence' easily wins out over the nature of the facts.

This is a phenomenon of perspectivization of a new kind, which makes itself felt today through the power of the instantaneous emission and reception of signals. These are currently analogue, but will soon give way to the digital, as the data which make up information undergo temporal compression.

Thus what is now put into perspective is not so much space as time. This is no longer the time of the *longues durées* of the chronicles of yesteryear, but the time of light and its speed – a *cosmological constant* capable of conditioning human history.

To the three geometrical dimensions which previously determined the perception of the relief of real space is now added *the third dimension of matter itself*: after 'mass' and 'energy', the dimension of 'information' makes its entry into the history of reality, overlaying the real presence of things and places through the tele-surveillance and monitoring of the environment.

At that point, far from setting the **actual** perspective of optical presence of the Quattrocento against the **virtual** perspective of electro-optic tele-presence, *the real-time perspective* of telecommunications combines the two, thus creating a 'field effect' in which the actual and the virtual together produce a new kind of **relief**, not unlike the 'soundscape' of hi-fi with its treble and bass notes.

The material and geometrical volume of an object is then succeeded by the immaterial and electronic volume of information; acoustic and visual information, but also tactile information, through the virtual reality gauntlet, and olfactory information with the recent invention of digitized chemical sensors.

After the stereophonic and stereoscopic effects we have known, audiovisual **representation** is at last opening up to the artifice of a **presentation** of reality that is both accelerated and augmented: the 'stereo-reality' of a world without any apparent horizon in which the *frame of the screen* has taken over from the distant horizon *line*. This square horizon of the computer terminal or head-mounted screen (HMS) presents, like certain kinds of spectacles, the very latest 'volume' – no longer that of things perceptible to the naked eye, but of the *instantaneous superimposition of actual and virtual images.*

A de-localized perception, like our perception of the volume of the hologram, which augments any perceptible reality, but does so by *accelerating* it to the limit-velocity of the propagation of the electromagnetic waves which carry the various information signals.

The conflict which rested on the geometric division between the opposites of Right and Left gives way to the axis of stereoscopic symmetry of that *real-time perspective* which revolutionizes historical time and the culture of nations by converting all present reality into wave form.

Thus, just as the European Renaissance is unimaginable without the invention of the perspective of real space and of Galileo's telescope, so geopolitical globalization will be inseparable from the unification of this real-time perspective and this new spatio-temporal relief that is a product of the electromagnetic radiation of telecommunications.

After the era of the *energy-based* acceleration of steam and internal combustion engines, or of the electric engine, comes the age of the *cyber-acceleration* of the very latest engines: the 'logical inference' engine of the computer and its software, the 'reality' engine of virtual space and the 'search engine' of the Internet in which computational speed succeeds the speed of the turbo-compressor of the automobile engine, or the speed of the turbines and jets of supersonic flight. The absolute speed of the new means of telematic transmission coming in their turn to dominate the relative speed of the old means of transport, the local acceleration of vehicles ceding its primacy to the general acceleration of the vectors of an information that is going global.

It is easy to see, then, that de-localization is not merely

a phenomenon of post-industrial business,[1] but a phenomenon of the **appearance business**, of the grand-scale cybernetic optics which is capable of *presenting the whole world for our inspection by virtue of the transparency of appearances instantly transmitted over a distance.*

This is a means of transport for everyone's eyes, a *telescopy*, the product of an electro-optic and acoustic propagation which complements the direct transparency of *matter* – such as that of air, water or glass – with the indirect transparency of *light* and its speed.

Thus, after the development of the transport networks in the nineteenth and twentieth centuries, with the network of networks, the Internet, comes the imminent establishment of real *networks of transmission of the vision of the world*, the audiovisual information superhighways of those on-line cameras which will contribute, in the twenty-first century, to developing the **panoptical** (and permanent) tele-surveillance of planetary sites and activities, which will very probably end in the implementation of networks of virtual reality. This is a **cyberoptics** which will leave intact neither the old *aesthetics* that was a product of European modernity, nor the *ethics* of the Western democracies.

I am referring to that 'representative democracy', which tomorrow will be subject to the pressure of the acceleration of historical reality, with the incalculable risk that the

---

1 The French '*délocalisation*' has become synonymous with the relocation of the production plants of multinational companies in more profitable parts of the world, which has characterized the recent period of post-industrial development in Europe. (Trans.)

'commerce of the visible' will bring about what no totalitarian regime has managed to create through ideology: *unanimous support.*

A slow and measured democracy, locally situated, in the style of the direct democracy of the assemblies of the Swiss cantons, or a 'live', media democracy, on the lines of the measurement of audience ratings in commercial television or the opinion poll? Ultimately, it is the whole problem of *immediacy* and *instantaneity* in politics that is posed today. After *the authority of human beings* over their history, are we going to yield, with the acceleration of the real, to the *authority of machines* and those who programme them? Shall we see the mechanical transference of the power of the political parties to the power of electronic or other devices?

After the disasters of technocracy, are we going to go from the frying pan into the fire by yielding to the social **cybernetics** so dreaded by the inventors of automation? Are we going to cede the administration of life to inanimate but ultra-rapid devices which are capable of scaling the heights of technical progress? To espouse that (virtual) *automatic democracy*, the practical efficacy of which is confined solely to the time saved in announcing election results? In fact, with the acquisition of the *global speed* of telecommunications, as opposed to the *local speed* of our previous 'means of communication', we are moving towards inertia, towards the sterility of movement.

Every time we introduce an acceleration, not only do we reduce the expanse of the world, but we also sterilize movement and the grandeur of movement by rendering useless the act of the locomotor body. Similarly, we lose the mediating value of 'action', while that of the immediacy of 'interaction' gains in comparison.

In this way great speeds are gradually replacing the great expanses, and the surface – the immense surface areas of the terrestrial globe – is giving way to the interface of global speed.

This is precisely what 'live action' is: the 'real time' of globalization. In that process, the *light of speed* supplants the light of the sun and the alternation of day and night. The electromagnetic radiation of waves wins out over the sun's rays and the shadows they cast, to the point where the *local day* of calendar time abandons its historical importance to the *global day* of universal time.

One example, among others, of the disqualification of all distance – and hence of all genuine action – is that of the ocean, of all the world's oceans, with the appearance of the supersonic speed of aviation. Or alternatively, and more simply, we have the example of the 'grand staircase', which, with the appearance of the lift, became the 'service stairs' or the 'emergency exit'.

Just as the Atlantic and the Pacific are merely maritime expanses disqualified by the great atmospheric speeds achieved as aeronautics has supplanted sea travel, every time we introduce a higher speed we discredit the value of an action, alienating our power to act for the sake of our power to react, which is another, less elevated name for what we currently term 'interaction'.

But this is as nothing beside the coming introduction of the 'automatable processing of knowledge', that generalization of amnesia which will be the ultimate achievement of the *oblivion industry*, since the sum total of analogue information (audiovisual and other) should soon be replaced by the digital, with computer codes taking over from the language of 'words and things'.

Figures are thus readying themselves to reign in their mathematical omnipotence, the *instrument of number* is preparing to dominate the *analogon* once and for all – in other words, to dominate anything which presents a resemblance, or relations of similitude, between beings and things.

This leads, self-evidently, to the denial of any *phenomenology*. Far from wishing to 'save phenomena', as philosophy demanded, we shall henceforth have to mislay them, to lose them beneath calculations, beneath the speed of a calculation which outstrips any time of thought, any intelligent reflection.

In this field, the crisis of contemporary art is in fact merely a clinical symptom of the crisis of contemporaneity itself – one indicator among many others of the break in temporality which lies before us.

At the end of the twentieth century, art no longer speaks of the past or represents the future; it is becoming the privileged instrument of the present and simulaneity. As an 'art of presence', ranged against the industry of telepresence, and in the face of the coming of the 'live', contemporary art has stopped representing the figure of the world so as to present its 'reality' – first through the denial of all figuration in the European abstraction of the immediate post-war period; then, conversely, with American hyper-realism. Still to come was that sudden motorization of computer-generated images, which had been prefaced by video-art and its de-localized installations – not to mention that origin of 'motor art' already represented by cinema at the end of the nineteenth century.

But let us come to the *body* and its real presence in the theatre and in contemporary dance, in the age of the emergence of virtual reality. Curiously, temporality has now become a *topical subject* and a new form of theatrical – and other – action.

As a punctual form of 'time compression', historicity shrinks away to nothing now, being in the end a mere 'citation', a gradually reducing relic, in which unfolding time becomes a kind of 'present continuous', a perpetual present.

'We then find the loss of that founding element of theatrical fiction termed the *unity of time*, made up of a beginning, a middle and an end,' wrote Hans-Thies Lehmann, a specialist in contemporary dramaturgy. And he went on:

> This is done in order to establish the dimension of *time shared*, in all senses of the term *hic et nunc*, by actors and audience. To such a point that it can happen, in this perspective, that actual duration ceases to apply, with all events remaining suspended, strictly centred on the *nunc* and the present of its immediate now-ness to the detriment of the *hic*, the 'here' of the scene – of any 'scene' or any 'act'.[2]

Here no longer exists; everything is **now**, as we put it above.

---

2 From a version of a text published as 'Time Structures/Time Sculptures', *Theaterschrift* 12, December 1997, pp. 28–47.

The new 'theatrical representation', characteristic of the perspective of the time of the acceleration of the real and its *relief*, attempts uneasily to react to the *hurried presentation* of events by the media of mass communication, all of which favour the 'scoop' and the 'sound-bite' over the narrative and its unbearable '*longueurs*'. The aim is to avoid at all costs the remote-control handset coming into play, that sudden *symmetry-breaking* between transmitter and receiver.

Deterring theatre from being theatre – in other words, from showing a body (on the stage) in the era of the fiction of virtual-reality clones and avatars (on the screen) – this is the new 'paradox of the actor' (Diderot).

The dramaturgy of real time is, in fact, everywhere today: in the precariousness of the job market, fixed-term contracts or long-term unemployment; in families broken and reconstructed by succeeding divorces . . . The fear of zapping is becoming universal.

If the 'present' is indeed the *axis of symmetry* of passing time, this **omnipresent** centre now controls the totality of the life of the 'advanced' societies and we have at all costs to avoid the 'breaking' of that axis, which would lead back to the 'past', to dead memory and – who knows? – to remorse. Have we not in recent years seen the emergence of a vogue for repentance, a wave of guiltless officials apologizing for offences committed by their predecessors, but less worried, it would seem, about the crimes they may currently be committing? Or, alternatively, we must avoid that sudden temporal 'symmetry-breaking' which could project us into the future – something we have been partially cured of by the failures of economic planning.

'No future' is indeed the slogan which suits the relief of the 'real time' of this globalization, in which *everything arrives without there being any need to depart*, to move towards the beings around us, the surrounding places and things.

Whereas formerly, in the age of the transport revolution, the length of journeys and the scope of physical movement meant that moments of arrival were limited, in the age of the transmission revolution everything comes straight in, arrives immediately, given a general absence of delay, instantaneity of information and the development of that **interaction** which surpasses any **action**, any concrete act.

The *actual reality* of communications, supplanted by the *virtual reality* of telecommunications, then falls into a discredit comparable to that which in the past hit the world's oceans – *those stretches* of nautical miles now polluted as much by aeronautical speed as they are by the oil tankers sluicing out their tanks which has turned them into a sewage farm.

Thus, just as the 'heavier-than-air' mode of aviation is based, thanks to rapidity of propulsion, on *mere wind*, so our 'accelerated reality' is based on the 'lift' provided by the propagation of waves conveying signals instantaneously.

The history of the end of this millennium, held in a levitated state, is based almost solely on the incessant *tele-presence* of events which do not really succeed each other, since the **relief** of instantaneity is already winning out over the **depth** of historical successivity.

Finally, everything is reversed. What arrives, what suddenly comes to us is far more important than what leaves, what goes off to the depths of our memories or the far reaches of the apparent geographical horizon. Hence the decline, which is so revealing, of theatrical representation, the concrete fiction of which stands opposed, by the actor's *being there*, to the discrete fiction of the electromagnetic spectres which fill our screens.

In these last performances, the unhappy attempt 'is also made in some forms of theatre to absorb and outdo the speed of the media. . . . Lines are delivered in such rapid succession that you get the impression of the kind of speed and abrupt transitions usually associated with channel-surfing or zapping.'[3]

The 'acts' of the play then become 'inter-acts', if not indeed 'inter-vals', in which actor and spectator cease to be different in nature. We have the fusion/confusion of 'roles' or, more exactly, the superfusion [*surfusion*] of the scenic fiction of the theatre and that of the past-less and future-less moment of virtual reality. The **drip-feed** [*surfusion*] of a body whose state has ceased to respond to the outer conditions of the stage, but still has its physical equilibrium maintained most precariously, as the Accident which will unfailingly bring down this house of cards is temporarily staved off.

How can we avoid mentioning once again here the emblematic example of the 'financial scene' and its speculative bubble, that virtual bubble of a planetary economy which is based today on the automatic interaction between market prices, which bear no relation whatever to the real wealth of the production of nations? And the implementation, a dozen or so years ago, of 'program trading', which automated the actions of the players, the traders on Wall

---

3 Ibid., p. 41.

Street and the other stock exchanges, and also that speculative Big Bang, soon to be followed by the crash of '87,
which subsequently meant that what amounted to 'circuit
breakers' had to be put in to prevent the system running
out of control? A form of channel-hopping aimed at pre-
venting the reorganization of local financial markets into a
single global market from producing a repetition of that
'accident'. It did not, however, prevent the Asian crash of
autumn 1997.

There again, the 'dramaturgy of real time' can be seen
to have played its fateful role, depriving the economic
actors of the thinking time essential to rational action.

It is the same, in the end, in the cultural field, with the
collapse of the 'art market', which has not just triggered a
collapse in the relative importance of particular, clearly
over-rated artists, but has also gravely compromised the
very reality of the values of contemporary art. To confirm
this, one has only to follow the burgeoning debates in
Europe on the crisis in art, of the kind which take place,
for example, around major events such as the last
Documenta at Kassel.

After the acceleration of the history of so-called classical art in the period when 'modern art' was emerging, we
now have the acceleration of the reality of so-called contemporary art and the appearance of an '*art actuel*' which is
apparently attempting to counter the impending arrival of
a *virtual art*, the age of **cyberculture**.

Extending the dislocation of the figure, which we saw at
the beginning of the twentieth century with Cubism, and
its disappearance into forms of abstraction, geometric or
otherwise, de-localization – the product of the age of the
virtual – leads today to an art of interactive feedback

between the artist and his/her visitors, along the lines of those infographic paintings which change and metamorphose as you contemplate them, doing so from the particular viewpoint of each of the actors/spectators. Moreover, the *decomposition* of figures in Pointillism or Divisionism leads today, thanks to fractal geometry, to another type of deconstruction: the dismantling of the space-time of the work.

In the age of the sudden *electronic motorization* of the artwork, dislocation of forms and de-localization of the art object go hand in hand and accompany the acceleration not in this case of history, but of the *reality of the plastic arts*. This represents, on the one hand, a questioning of the roles of actor and spectator, and, on the other, an interrogation of the notions of author and viewer. And it is a calling into question of the *site of art*, after the questioning of the site of the theatrical scene. These are all so many harbingers of an unprecedented change – premonitory signs of the new time scheme within which culture will operate in the era of the emergence of cyberculture.

CHAPTER 14

With the end of the twentieth century, it is not merely the second millennium which is reaching its close. The Earth too, the planet of the living, is being closed off.

Globalization is not so much, then, the *accomplishment* of the acceleration of history as the *completion*, the closure, of the field of possibilities of the terrestrial horizon.

The Earth is now double-locked by the endless round of satellites and we are running up against the invisible outer wall of habitable space, in the same way as we bump up against the envelope, the firm flesh, of a liveable body. As mere men and women, mere terrestrials, the world for us today is a dead-end and claustrophobia an agonizing threat. Our metaphysical hopes have wasted away and our desires for physical emancipation are similarly withered.

The Earth of the great multiplication of the species is becoming, then, the colony, the camp of the great ordeal. Babel is returning – as cosmic ghetto, city and world all in one – and perhaps this time it is indestructible.

Less than a thousand days before the end of a pitiless

century, a series of facts, of events of all kinds, alerts us to an untimely emergence of limits, the end of a geophysical horizon which had till then set the tone of history.

Between the astrophysical suicide of the Heaven's Gate sect and the Assumption of Princess Diana, we had the announcement, the official annunciation of the genetic bomb, the unprecedented possibility of cloning human beings on the basis of a computer read-out of the map of the human genome.

Since then, thanks to the coupling of the life and information sciences, the outlines of a **cybernetic eugenicism** have emerged, a eugenicism which owes nothing to the politics of nations – as was still the case in the laboratories of the death camps – but everything, absolutely everything, to science – an economic techno-science in which the single market demands the commercialization of the whole of living matter, the privatization of the genetic heritage of humanity. Besides this, the proliferation of atomic weapons, freshly boosted by India, Pakistan and probably other destabilized countries on the Asian continent, is prompting the United States – the last great world power – to accelerate its famous 'revolution in military affairs' by developing that emergent strategy known as 'information war', which consists in using electronics as a hegemonic technology: a role it now takes over from nuclear physics.

The atom bomb can then be merely a last guarantee, provided of course that the information bomb effectively proves its credentials as the new absolute weapons system.

It is in this context of financial instability and military uncertainty, in which it is impossible to differentiate between information and disinformation, that the question of the **integral accident** arises once again and that we learn, at the Birmingham summit of May 1998, that the Central Intelligence Agency not only takes seriously the possibility of a 'widespread computer catastrophe' in the year 2000, but that it has scheduled this hypothetical event into its calendar, indicating on a state-by-state basis how far individual nations still have to go to forearm themselves against it.[1]

Similarly, the United States Senate announced the creation of a committee to assess this potential electronic disaster and the Bank of International Settlements in New York followed suit shortly afterwards, setting up a high-level committee to attempt to forestall a **computer crash** in which the damage caused by the serial downturns in the Asian economies might produce global meltdown.

As the first great global manoeuvre in 'Information Warfare',[2] what we see here is the launch of a new logistics, that of the cybernetic control of knowledge: politico-economic knowledge, in which the single market affords a glimpse of its military and strategic dimension in terms of 'information transfer'. To the point where the *systemic risk* of a chain reaction of the bankruptcy of the financial markets (for so long masked during the promotional launch of the Internet) is now officially acknowledged, showing that this *major risk* can also be used to exert pressure on those nations which are reluctant to give in to free-trade blackmail.[3]

---

1 Michel Alberganti, 'Un problème majeur pour la communauté internationale', *Le Monde*, 21 May 1998.
2 In English in the original. (Trans.)
3 As with the Multilateral Agreement on Investment and the New Transatlantic Market.

As I pointed out some considerable time ago, if *interactivity* is to information what *radioactivity* is to energy, then we are confronted with the fearsome emergence of the 'Accident to end all accidents', an accident which is no longer *local* and precisely situated, but *global* and generalized. We are faced, in other words, with a phenomenon which may possibly occur everywhere simultaneously.

But what we might add today is that this *global systemic risk* is precisely what makes for the strategic supremacy of the future 'weapons systems' of the infowar, that electro-economic war declared on the world by the United States and that, far more than the viruses and other 'logical bombs' hidden away by hackers in the software of our computers, this **integral accident** is the true detonator of the **information bomb**, and hence of its future power of deterrence over the political autonomy of nations.

As the ultimate exemplar of monopoly, the **cyberworld** is thus never anything else but the hypertrophied form of a cybernetic colonialism, with the interconnectedness of the Internet prefiguring the imminent launch of the **cyberbomb** – the future information superhighways – and, subsequently, the establishment, still under the aegis of the United States, not just of an expanded NATO but also of *new all-out defences* on the Cold War model, with cyber-glaciation here supplanting nuclear deterrence.

On 12 May 1998, again at the meeting of heads of state in Birmingham, the American president, in his report on 'the strategy for controlling cybernetic crime', stressed the urgent need to establish legislation against the **cybercrime** of mafias using remote technologies and also against the risks involved in the emergence of 'digital money', 'e-cash', which too easily evades any economic control.

'Cybercriminals can use computers to raid our banks . . . extort money by threats to unleash computer viruses,' declared Bill Clinton,[4] explaining to the heads of state present that the United States was in the front line of the battle against this, but that 'international crime requires an international response. America is prepared to act alone when it must, *but no nation can control cybercrime by itself any more.*'[5]

It is hard to believe one's ears. The president of the state responsible for the greatest economic deregulation in history still seeks to pose as the first person daring to shout 'fire!' so as to lead a crusade against a chaos he himself has organized, together with his vice-president, prime mover in the creation of the future information superhighways.

The atom bomb, the information bomb and the demographic bomb – these three historical deflagrations evoked by Albert Einstein in the early 1960s are now on the agenda for the next millennium. The first is there, with the dangers of nuclear weapons becoming generally commonplace, as heralded in the Indian and Pakistani nuclear tests. And the second is also present, with the threat of

---

4 Aurélien Daudet, 'Les chefs d'État contre le cybercrime', *Le Figaro*, 16/17 May 1998. The full text of this part of the speech, as published by the White House, reads: 'As Agent Riley's remarks suggest, cybercriminals can use computers to raid our banks, run up charges on our credit cards, extort money by threats to unleash computer viruses'. (Trans.)

5 Ibid. The text of the speech as released by the White House refers simply to 'crime' here, not to 'cybercrime' as in *Le Figaro*'s report. The italics are Paul Virilio's. (Trans.)

cybernetic control of the politics of states, under the indirect threat of a *generalized accident*, as we have seen above.

As for the third, the *demographic bomb*, it is clear that if the use of computers is indispensable in the development of atomic weapons, it is equally indispensable in the decipherment of the genetic code and hence in the research aimed at drawing up *a physical map of the human genome*, thus opening up a new eugenicism promoting not the *natural* but the *artificial* selection of the human species.[6]

And given the considerable growth in the demography of our planet in the twenty-first century, are we not right to suspect that experiments on the *industrialization of living matter* will not be content merely to treat patients and assist infertile couples to have children, but will soon lead back to that old folly of the 'new man'? That is to say, the man who will deserve to survive (the superman), whereas the man without qualities, the primate of the new times, will have to disappear – just as the 'savage' had to disappear in the past to avoid cluttering up a small planet – and give way to the latest model of humanity, the **transhuman**, built on the lines of transgenic crops, which are so much better adapted to their environment than the natural products. That this is indeed the case is confirmed by the recent declarations of Professor Richard Seed on his attempt to achieve human cloning, or the statements of those who

---

6 While Darwin, in *The Origin of Species*, had advanced the principle of the natural selection of the individuals fittest to survive, in 1860 his cousin, Francis Galton, proposed the principle of artificial selection or, in other words, a voluntary policy of the elimination of the least fit, thus institutionalizing the struggle against the alleged degeneracy of the human species.

openly advocate the production of *living mutants*, which are likely to hasten the coming, after the extra-terrestrial, of the extra-human, another name for the superhuman race which still looms large in our memories.

And is the 'human genome project', which has now been running for ten years and which is financed to the tune of $3 billion by the Department of Energy and the National Institute of Health for the purpose of deciphering DNA, anything other than a race at last to acquire the *data of life*, just as, in another age, the United States aimed for the moon by financing NASA?

It is always a race! Has not the geneticist Graig Venter just set up a private company with the aim of deciphering, in a project parallel to the public one, the whole of the genetic code *in just three years*, by linking up with a subsidiary of the pharmaceuticals group Perkin Elmer, who are specialists in DNA-sequencing machines, and doing this with an investment of just $200 million?[7]

After Kasparov's symbolic failure against the Deep Blue computer, the summer saga of the automatic Mars Pathfinder probe and the misadventures of the Mir space station, we are seeing the scheduled end of *manned flight* and a questioning of even the usefulness of the future international orbital station. This is the end of an 'extra-terrestrial' adventure for our generation but we have before us, by contrast, the spectacular launch of the 'extra-human' epic, as astrophysics gradually gives way to biophysics.

---

7 Fabrice Nodé Langlois, '"Coup d'accélérateur" dans la course aux gènes', *Le Figaro*, 16/17 May 1998.

These are all so many signs of the imminent supplanting of macro-physical *exoticism* by micro-physical *endoticism*. A probable end to the external colonization of the space of distant lands and the dubious dawning of a colonization which will be internal – the colonization of the space-time of living matter, the new frontier of the will to power of the techno-sciences.

'*Homo est clausura mirabilium dei*', wrote Hildegard of Bingen, thus expressing a reality previously masked by the anthropocentrism of origins: man might not be said to be the *centre of the world*, but its closure, the *end of the world*. Significantly, this phrase was uttered by a woman born in the year 1098. It is a phrase which stands opposed to the eugenic myth by throwing a singular light on the origin of nihilism in the *omnipotence of the impotence* of sciences as soon as they reopen the question of the origins of life.

Genetic engineering is fundamentally eugenicist, but only the memory of the Nazi extermination requires it to admit this. Hence the seriousness of the *negationist threat*, not just against the prophetic memory of the death camps but against the principle of the continuity of the living, that 'principle of responsibility' towards the future of humanity.

This is a shamefully 'conservative' principle in the eyes of those who desire nothing so much as *the revolution of the end*, that nihilism of an omnipotent progress which runs through the twentieth century from the *Titanic* to Chernobyl, with an eye always to the coming of the **Survivor**, the messiah so fervently desired by the cult of madness of present times.

In fact, since the end of the Cold War we have been constantly trying to reproduce other ends on this identical pattern: the end of history, the end of representative democracy or, again, the end of the subject, by attempting to create the *double* (the clone) or the *hybrid* (the mutant) thanks to genetic manipulation.

Far from being some kind of achievement, this 'post-industrial' undertaking deploys *the energy of despair* in an effort to escape the conditions favourable to life and thus to arrive at chaos, or, in other words, to regress to the initial conditions which prevailed, as it is believed, before the origins of life.

Transgenic, transhuman – these are all terms which mark the headlong charge forward, in spite of all the evidence, of a *transpolitical* community of scientists solely preoccupied with acrobatic performances. In this they are following the example of those fairground shows mounted in the nineteenth century by the self-styled 'mathemagicians' . . .

Ultimately, this so-called post-modern period is not so much the age in which industrial modernity has been surpassed, as the era of the sudden *industrialization of the end*, the all-out globalization of the havoc wreaked by progress.

To attempt to industrialize living matter by *bio-technological* procedures, as is done in the semi-official project of reproducing the individual in standard form, is to *turn the end into an enterprise*, into a Promethean factory.

In the age of the 'balance of nuclear terror' between East and West, the military-industrial complex had already succeeded in militarizing scientific research to ensure the capability of mutual destruction – the 'MAD' concept. *Genetic* engineering is now taking over from the *atomic* industry to invent *its own* bomb.

Thanks to computers and the advances of bio-technology, the life sciences are able to threaten the species no longer (as in the past) by the radioactive destruction of the human environment, but by clinical insemination, by the control of the sources of life, the origin of the individual.

We can see now that, just as the total war outlined at the end of the First World War was to be actualized during the Second, threatening, between 1939 and 1945, with Hiroshima and Auschwitz, not the *enemy* but the human race, the **global warfare** prefigured today in the great manoeuvres of 'information warfare' will be based on a scientific radicalization, threatening – not so much with extermination as with extinction – not a particular population or even the human race (as the thermo-nuclear bomb might), but the very principle of all individuated life, the *genetic* and *information* bombs now forming a single 'weapons system'.

Moreover, if information is indeed *the third dimension* of matter, after mass and energy, each historical conflict has in its time shown up the mastery of these elements. *Mass war*: from the great ancient invasions to the organization of the firepower of armies during the recent European wars. *Energy war*: with the invention of gunpowder and, most significantly, of atomic weapons, with the 'advanced' or high-energy laser still to come. And lastly, tomorrow, *the information war*, which will make general what espionage and police surveillance inaugurated long ago, though they were unable to draw, as we are today, on the limit-acceleration of 'global information'.

'He who knows everything fears nothing,' declared Joseph Goebbels, the head of the Propagandastaffel. In fact, here as elsewhere, the question is not so much one of fearing as of *spreading fear* by the permanent over-exposure of

life, of all lives, to 'all-out' control, which is a *fait accompli* –
or almost – thanks to computer technology. But let us go
back for a moment to the third dimension of organized
matter: whether it be speed of acquisition, transmission or
computation, *information is inseparable from its acceleration in
energy terms* – slowed-up information being no longer even
worthy of that name, but mere background noise.

As we may recall, a journalist at the time of the creation
of CNN offered the thought: 'Slow news, no news?'

In fact the limit-speed of the waves which convey messages and images *is the information itself*, irrespective of its
content, to the point where Marshall McLuhan's famous
formula has to be corrected: 'it is not the *medium* which is
the message, but merely *the velocity* of the medium'. An
ultimate and absolutely final velocity, which has just tele-
scoped the 'time barrier', while tomorrow the photonic
computer will calculate in perfect synchronism with the
speed of light, which today promotes instantaneous
telecommunications.

The 'information war' will soon be based, then, on
global interactivity, just as the war of atomic energy was
based on *local radioactivity* – and this will be so to the point
that it will be entirely impossible to distinguish a deliberate
action from an involuntary reaction or an 'accident'; or to
distinguish an attack from a mere technical breakdown, as
was already the case on 19 May 1998 (synchronizing almost
perfectly with the Birmingham summit) when the Galaxy
IV telecommunications satellite suddenly interrupted the
messages of some 40 million American pager devotees after
the device's on-board computer had slightly shifted the
satellite's position. *An unforeseen accident or a full-scale test for
infowar?*

It is impossible to be certain, but the affair immediately triggered a debate on the vulnerability of the USA to breakdowns in a technology essential to the life of the country.[8]

As one might imagine, the Internet, the direct descendant of Arpanet, helped to keep certain American public services up and running, such as the NPR radio channel which resorted to the Net to re-establish the link with some of its 600 local stations.

We should not forget that the cybernetic system of the Web was set in place more than twenty years ago to counter the electromagnetic effects of an atomic explosion at altitude and thus to forestall a generalized accident affecting strategic telecommunications.

If war has always been the invention of new types of destruction, the promotion of a series of deliberately provoked accidents (the 'war machine' is only ever the inversion of the productive machine), with the infowar which is currently in preparation the very notion of 'accident' is taken to extremes, with the extraordinary possibility of a *generalized accident* which, like a cluster bomb, would embrace a very great range of accidents of all kinds.

Not a local accident, as in the past, but a global one, capable of halting the life of a continent, if not indeed of several at once, as with the threat to the operation of our computers on the eve of the year 2000.

In the field of information warfare, everything is, then, hypothetical; and just as information and disinformation have become indistinguishable from each other, so have

---

8 'Un satellite qui dévie et c'est l'Amérique qui déraille', *Libération*, 22 May 1998.

attacks and mere accidents . . . And yet the message here is not *scrambled*, as was still the case with the counter-measures in electronic warfare; it has become **cybernetic**. That is to say, the 'information' is not so much the explicit content as the rapidity of its feedback.

Interactivity, immediacy, ubiquity – this is the true message of transmission and reception *in real time*.

Digital messages and images matter less than their instantaneous delivery; the 'shock effect' always wins out over the consideration of the informational content. Hence the indistinguishable and therefore unpredictable character of the offensive act and the technical breakdown.

The indeterminacy principle then spreads from the quantum world to that of a computerized information strategy which is independent – or almost independent – of the conditions of the geophysical milieu where its effects are nonetheless felt.

Thanks to the patient establishment of an interactivity extended to the whole of our planet, 'information warfare' is preparing the first world war of time or, more precisely, *the first war of world time*, of that 'real time' of exchanges between the interconnected networks.

We can easily see, then, that the current globalization of the market also has three dimensions to it: *geophysical*, *techno-scientific* and *ideological*. Hence the inevitable connection to be made between the United States's resolve to aim for global free trade by the period 2010–20[9] and the preparations for an information war.

---

9 Martine Laronche, 'Quelles limites au libre-échange?', *Le Monde*, 26 May 1998.

It is, in fact, impossible clearly to distinguish *economic* war from *information* war, since each involves the same hegemonic ambition of making commercial and military exchanges interactive.[10]

Hence the repeated efforts of the World Trade Organization (WTO) to deregulate the various different national sovereignties with the MAI, the Multilateral Agreement on Investment, or, alternatively, with European Commissioner Leon Brittan's New Transatlantic Market.

One would in the end understand nothing of the *systematic* deregulation of the market economy if one did not connect it with the *systemic* deregulation of strategic information.

To render all exchanges **cybernetic**, whether they be peaceful or belligerent, is the discreet aim of the contemporary innovations of the end of this millennium. But here the very last 'fortress' is no longer the Europe of the EEC so much as the living human being – that isolated 'human planet', which has at all costs to be invaded or captured through the industrialization of living matter.

Let us sum up: yesterday's was a *totalitarian war*, in which the dominant elements were quantity, mass and the power of the atomic bomb. Tomorrow's war will be *globalitarian*, in which, by virtue of the information bomb, the qualitative will be of greater importance than geophysical scale or population size.

---

10 On the control of flows of commercial imagery by the Pentagon, see the development of the National Imagery and Mapping Agency (NIMA).

Not 'clean war' *with zero deaths*, but 'pure war' *with zero births* for certain species which have disappeared from the **bio**-diversity of living matter.[11] The warfare of tomorrow – and here it will be comparable with the 'desk murders' of yesteryear – will not be so much an affair of desks as of laboratories – of laboratories with their doors flung wide to the radiant future of *transgenic* species, supposedly better adapted to the pollution of a small planet held in suspension in the ether of telecommunications.

---

11 Catherine Vincent, 'Les Suisses conviés à un choix de société sur les biotechnologies', *Le Monde*, 27 May 1998. For the first time a sovereign people was on 7 June 1998 to vote on the initiative 'for genetic protection' aimed at reinforcing regulation with regard to transgenic manipulation.

AVAILABLE IN THE RADICAL THINKERS SERIES

Minima Moralia:
Reflections on a
Damaged Life
THEODOR ADORNO

Paperback 1 84467 051 1
$12/£6/$14CAN
256 pages • 5 x 7.75 inches

For Marx
LOUIS ALTHUSSER

Paperback 1 84467 052 X
$12/£6/$14CAN
272 pages • 5 x 7.75 inches

The System of Objects
JEAN BAUDRILLARD

Paperback 1 84467 053 8
$12/£6/$14CAN
224 pages • 5 x 7.75 inches

Liberalism and Democracy
NORBERTO BOBBIO

Paperback 1 84467 062 7
$12/£6/$14CAN
112 pages • 5 x 7.75 inches

AVAILABLE IN THE RADICAL THINKERS SERIES

The Politics of Friendship
JACQUES DERRIDA

Paperback 1 84467 054 6
$12/£6/$14CAN
320 pages • 5 x 7.75 inches

The Function of Criticism
TERRY EAGLETON

Paperback 1 84467 055 4
$12/£6/$14CAN
136 pages • 5 x 7.75 inches

Signs Taken for Wonders:
On the Sociology of Literary
Forms

FRANCO MORETTI

Paperback 1 84467 056 2
$12/£6/$14CAN
288 pages • 5 x 7.75 inches

The Return of the Political
CHANTAL MOUFFE

Paperback 1 84467 057 0
$12/£6/$14CAN
176 pages • 5 x 7.75 inches

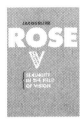

Printed in the United States
by Baker & Taylor Publisher Services